W9-BMV-441

1990

Capitalism, Communism
and Coexistence

Capitalism, Communism
and Coexistence

From the Bitter Past to a Better Prospect

**John Kenneth Galbraith
and Stanislav Menshikov**

HAMISH HAMILTON · LONDON

HAMISH HAMILTON LTD

Published by the Penguin Group
27 Wrights Lane, London w8 5tz, England
Viking Penguin Inc, 40 West 23rd Street, New York, New York 10010, U.S.A.
Penguin Books Australia Ltd, Ringwood, Victoria, Australia
Penguin Books Canada Ltd, 2801 John Street, Markham, Ontario, Canada l3r 1b4
Penguin Books (N.Z.) Ltd, 182-190 Wairau Road, Auckland 10, New Zealand

Penguin Books Ltd, Registered Offices: Harmondsworth, Middlesex, England

First published in Great Britain 1989 by
Hamish Hamilton Ltd
First published in U.S.A. 1988 by
Houghton Mifflin Company, Boston, Mass.

Copyright © 1988 by John Kenneth Galbraith

1 3 5 7 9 10 8 6 4 2

British Library Cataloguing in Publication Data
Galbraith, John Kenneth, *1908–*
Capitalism, communism and coexistence.
1. Western bloc countries. Foreign relations
with communist countries   2. Communist
countries. Foreign relations with Western
bloc countries
I. Title   II. Menshikov, S.M. (Stanislav
Mikhailovich)
327′.90171′3

isbn 0-241-12608-8

Printed in Great Britain by
Butler & Tanner Ltd, Frome and London

Contents

Contents

Introduction to the British Edition

One of the important, indeed all but inescapable, developments of our time is the declining power of stern, controlling ideology in public affairs. This is certainly so in the United States: the hard right of Ronald Reagan, or more precisely of his supporters, has come sharply into conflict with modern reality, a reality that accords an inescapable role to the state, not least in the bailing out of business organizations that have run into trouble and are too large to be allowed to fail. Or, against all conservative theology, in the sustaining of overall economic activity with an unprecedented peacetime budget deficit. Or, however reluctantly, in the inescapable pressures of the welfare state.

Similarly, the liberal left has come to accept and affirm an indispensable role for the market. And to assess public ownership and public regulation in a practical way.

One sees, or anyhow senses, the same trend in the United Kingdom — a trend that has divided the left as between pragmatic adaptation and still-firm ideological commitment. If Mrs. Thatcher has yielded less to pragmatism than Mr. Reagan has, it is because she is considerably more committed in personal belief and, one judges, also substantially more rugged in both leadership and administration.

The change here noted (France being another prominent example) has extended beyond the Western countries to the Soviet Union. There the question is how many concessions can be made to personal and group incentives and to market guidance of the economy without sacrificing the seventy-year-old commitment to socialism. And how, in turn, the great bureaucratic apparatus of socialism can be made more responsive in face of the power implicit in its existence.

It is this present-day trend that Stanislav Menshikov and I met to discuss at my farmstead in Vermont, intending, as has happened, that the results would be published more or less simultaneously in the United States and the U.S.S.R. Each afternoon we identified the subject for the next day's interchange. Each following morning we had, not without some prior thought, the resulting discussion. Most of our sessions were with only a court reporter present; one public session was for a huge and very evidently interested audience from those otherwise tranquil country precincts.

It was not our purpose to score points against each other, to find agreement where agreement did not exist, to win or lose a debate. We did seek, though our success is for the reader to judge, to make our exchange as informative and interesting as possible and if there was amusement to be had, not to resist it. After our meetings were over, we kept all the original content, but more than a little editing was required to convert the spoken word into acceptable English or Russian prose.

Stanislav Menshikov and I have been friends for many years. I knew him first when he was a University of Moscow professor specializing on the Western economies. He was, thereafter, a senior staff member at the United Nations in New York and in later times a high official in the international section of the Communist Central Committee. Most recently, he has been at the *World Marxist Review* in Prague. His ability and willingness to express himself clearly on economic and political matters in the Soviet Union, which is here evident, did not, I may say, begin with *glasnost*. His participation made this enterprise especially agreeable for me, as I believe the reader will sense.

In the United States over these last many years anti-Communism has become part of our culture. In introducing the American edition of this book, I noted that in our country lives "have been invested in the proposition that all Soviet spokesmen are instruments of a larger authority and are, at best, endlessly deceptive. Those who contend with them are [likely to be] themselves deceived. Or [show that] they are dangerously naive." I added in a handsome way that I was tolerant of this reaction: "A lifetime of belief is involved and to be protected." I would like to think that British readers, in an older, more eclectic tradition, are less religiously motivated, that they share my own strong commitment to hearing voices from across the Churchillian curtain and to hoping that the curtain will continue to disintegrate. In this spirit I have a special pleasure in offering this small book to a British audience.

JOHN KENNETH GALBRAITH
June 1988

Introduction to the American Edition

Twenty-four years ago, I attended a meeting on cultural exchanges in Leningrad and Moscow; with my eminently respectable colleagues — David Rockefeller, Norton Simon, Norman Cousins, Buckminster Fuller — I went to a luncheon one day at Spaso House, the American Embassy Residence. My Russian companion at the table was Stanislav Menshikov, a remarkably informed scholar, who provided me with an acute commentary on the policies of the Khrushchev regime, which was then in what might be called early evening. He was almost equally informed on American economic affairs, which, I learned, he taught at the University of Moscow.

My acquaintance with Menshikov has continued from those days, with encounters in Moscow, in New York, where he was on the senior staff of the United Nations for six years, and in Cambridge and Vermont. When, somewhat to my surprise, two of my books — my memoirs and *The New Industrial State* — were sought by a Soviet publisher, I discovered that Menshikov had encouraged the publication and acted otherwise as my sponsor.

Our most recent meeting was for some ten days in Vermont in the late summer of 1987. Each afternoon we met to consider our topic for the next morning; each morning we took up one of the subjects that gives title to one or more of the chapters in this book. Our plan was to have the result of these explorations published more or less simultaneously in the Soviet Union and the United States. This is happening. Our deeper purpose was to show that an American and a Russian of different views could engage in civil and, we hoped, informative discussions of our different and common problems. And of the terms and needs for our coexistence in a world that has become immutably and perilously interdependent and small. We also sought to deal with these great and solemn matters without being, in fact, too irretrievably solemn. A certain measure of detachment, even amusement, is not in conflict with the deeper claims of intelligence.

There were problems connected with our effort, as the reader will be aware. Our exchange took place last August. Book publishing, good book publishing, is a highly deliberate process. Much can happen before a volume finally appears in the stores. When we talked, the great stock market crash of October 19 had not occurred. Nor had the visit of General Secretary Gorbachev to Washington for the signing of the INF agreement and for the several meetings with diverse official and unofficial American groups, in one of which it was my pleasure to participate. All this, had it gone before, we would doubtless have discussed. But a book, as I've elsewhere noted, is not a newspaper or television commentary on yesterday's events. The subjects we chose to discuss have a durability that, I believe, survives the passing scene.

There are other, lesser matters that deserve a word. In these last decades anticommunism has become deeply a part of our culture. It has its own vested interest, not least in the scholarly or otherwise literate world. Lives have been invested in the proposition that all Soviet spokesmen are instruments of a larger authority and are, at best, endlessly deceptive. Those who contend with them are themselves deceived. Or they are dangerously naive.

My instinct is to be tolerant of this reaction. As I have said, a lifetime of belief is involved and to be protected. And there are individuals with larger interests — economic, military, bureaucratic — in continued tension with the Soviets. They too stand ready to criticize and condemn. But we are all, in some measure, the captives of our own past beliefs, our own community, our own interest. Thus my relaxed view. It is my personal conviction, amply if not adequately expressed in these pages, that civil discourse is essential in our time. Coexistence has its larger claim. And, to no one's astonishment, I do not believe that the advantage in discussion is all on one side.

But it was not our purpose, neither mine nor that of my Russian coauthor, to score points in our conversations. We did not see them as a debate in which either of us won or lost. We saw them rather as a contribution to the larger victory which equally we hope to share. That is our common well-being and survival.

JOHN KENNETH GALBRAITH
January 1988

1

Socialism in Light of Its History

JKG: It's very good to see you here in the United States and in Vermont again. May I assume that, as host, I have the privilege of asking the first question? Why is this an interesting and useful time to discuss American-Soviet relations and internal conditions in our two countries as they affect the world at large?

SM: I think that we're now at a turning point in the history of civilization. The most salient and extraordinary fact, a discovery which some have made only recently, is that a war between the United States and the Soviet Union, two major powers representing two different and competing social systems, could bring about an end to civilization and thus to both systems. It may be that this realization hasn't yet come home to many people, perhaps even to the majority. This is for various reasons. People have different and more pressing problems. Some in the world are hungry and thinking of food and survival on a much more mundane level. Others are in the midst of local civil warfare or wars to gain national sovereignty. And, in more stable and practical situations, some people are thinking primarily in terms of upward material or social mobility; for them also the nuclear threat seems to be distant.

JKG: I concur but would add one thing, something I've said often before: in the aftermath of nuclear war, the difference between capitalism and communism is not going to be evident even to the most committed ideologist.

More immediately, however, what of the changes that are taking place in the Soviet Union and perhaps in the United States? Don't these call for discussion at this particular time?

SM: Yes, I think that's true. But to finish the point I was developing: although most people perhaps don't realize yet that civilization may be threatened with extinction through nuclear war, that is the fact; and so the time has come for reassessment. We must look again at the relations between the two systems and the relations between the two countries. We must realize that nuclear war or no nuclear war, the systems are there, and even if we avoid direct confrontation, they will still be there. The systems won't cease to exist, so the problems between us will remain.

JKG: Let me press you on that. I agree that capitalism and communism will continue to exist, but isn't it true that we have come to a time when only those seriously afflicted with paranoia really imagine that communism — socialism — is going to take over in the United States or in the Western countries? And when it's equally foolish to imagine that the Soviet Union, whatever the changes now under way, is going to become a capitalist country?

SM: In order to answer that question, we should go deeper into what the conditions of the two systems are at the moment. But what I'm trying to say now is that both of our countries will have to learn to live together, and we must do that whether each thinks its system superior to the other or believes that its system will triumph in the end or not.

JKG: I agree, and no doubt we must also allow ourselves that sense of superiority that so rejoices us both.

But tell me, don't the more immediate changes make this an interesting time? The reforms introduced by Mr. Gorbachev come first to mind. Do you consider those changes decisively important?

SM: I think they are, in fact, revolutionary. Many of my countrymen talk about a second revolution like the October Revolution that occurred seventy years ago. We may agree or disagree with that particular point of view, but the fact is that the current changes are thought throughout the Soviet Union to be of a revolutionary nature and far-reaching.

JKG: This is something that our readers will want to hear more about from you. As for the United States, I don't think there are any changes under way at this time that are particularly decisive. But I have the feeling that perhaps we are on the verge of a new concern — a new search for solutions in areas in which capitalism, our system, is in default. I hope for a new concern for the unemployment in our big cities, the unemployment of minorities and the young in particular. And for the crisis in agriculture and in our older mass-production industries, which we now see become ossified, static. We have too many people who are homeless or ill housed. I think we're on the verge of recognizing these problems and others like them in a serious way. So perhaps one could say that while the Soviet Union has announced its revolution, we have ours around the corner.

SM: Yes. Whatever one thinks about one's own system and whether or not there is a general recognition that changes have to be made, the fact is that both capitalism and socialism are right now in the midst of a serious period of reassessment as a result of a crisis or precrisis situation. This is occurring in both societies, not just in socialism but in capitalism as well. Both have been successful and unsuccessful in many ways. But because of the realization of the possibility of nuclear war and the other major social problems in the world, such as the gap between the rich countries and the poor and the difficult relations between the superpowers and the smaller powers, we now know we must reassess. There is a crisis, and we really must change.

JKG: I think this is very important. But there is something else that bears heavily on our discussions. I remember in my past visits to your country, as you will remember from your many past visits to the United States, the tendency for those on each side to say, "We are the center of all virtue; you are the center of all evil." This doesn't allow for much useful discussion. Now I like to think we have reached a somewhat more mature stage in our respective develop- ments. Both of us can look candidly at our common prob- lems — such as the inefficiencies of our great industrial bureaucracies — and see how much we both still have to solve.

SM: I hope we will come to cooperate in the future, both the two countries and the two kinds of social system. Whether we're different, whether one is evil and the other virtuous, we will have to cooperate in things that concern us both, not just in the attempt to prevent nuclear war. Take the narcotics problem in the world.

JKG: Or alcoholism?

SM: Or the environment, or energy, or the population explosion and so on.

JKG: Or, as I've just said, the industrial bureaucracy. Or the difficulty of attracting people into low-prestige jobs. We both can recognize the fact that all people everywhere seek to avoid hard manual labor, the way you and I are avoiding it now.

But let me clarify one question for the sake of our future discussion. When we talk about the Soviet Union and the Soviet system, under what circumstances should we use the word "socialism" and when should we use the word "com- munism"? I've always been taught that communism is an ultimate, as yet unrealized condition, and when referring to the economy of the Soviet Union, we should call it socialism. Is that right?

SM: Yes, it is. In the Marxist view, socialism is a transitional phase from capitalism to communism. Communism is the future ideal society, which is distinguished by a super-abundance of goods and distribution that is practically free. Under socialism goods are distributed according to the labor input of each member of society.

JKG: Also under communism the state has withered away. I take it you don't insist that the state *has* withered away in the U.S.S.R.?

SM: No, but even when communism is achieved, the state may not wither away so completely. It all depends on what you consider the functions of the state. Let's try to go into this later — whether it's necessary to retain the functions of central planning in the future communist society.

JKG: You're saying that my recollection of Marx is a bit too literal?

SM: No. What I'm saying is that what Marx meant by the withering of the state might mean the withering of certain functions of the state, like the services of the police or the provision of defense if there is complete disarmament, for example. As far as economic management is concerned, however, the state might still have some functions.

JKG: I think you're modifying Marx for your own purposes, but that's entirely permissible. I have to concede that to a Marxist.

SM: Sometimes we have to modify.

But, seriously speaking, when we talk about reassessment, there's nothing bad about that. We should always reassess the theories on which we base our existence.

JKG: I surely agree. The notion that we are firmly tied to the ideas of the eighteenth and nineteenth centuries is something that no sensible man or woman can accept.

SM: Then there's another point, and that is that it's normal for any living system to undergo change from time to time; we have to experiment with new forms of organization so as to bring new vitality.

JKG: From what I remember of Marx, society is, in his words, in a constant process of transformation.

SM: That's true.

JKG: With that in mind, let us turn to the modern history of socialism and socialist economic development. It's now seventy years, give or take a few weeks, since the Russian Revolution and the arrival of socialism in Russia. How do you see socialism having changed since the days of Lenin?

SM: I want to start by saying that in the last seventy years socialism has shown itself to be a growing and vital system.

JKG: I would be surprised if you were to say it was a declining or immobile one.

SM: Some people, of course, *do* claim that socialism is in a process of general crisis, but let me substantiate my point a bit. Since 1917, socialism has developed in a number of countries, not in just one. Those countries are in Europe, Asia, the Americas and to some extent in Africa. The total number of people involved is quite large. About one third of the population of the world is now living under socialism. So you can consider it to be an international system on the same footing as capitalism, which encompasses two thirds of the world's population. One third is socialist; that's quite a large proportion.

JKG: I thought I noticed some hesitation in your voice when you mentioned countries in Africa — I assume Ethiopia and Mozambique — as socialist states. Marx would not have approved of socialism before there was capitalism, would he?

SM: Marx, of course, would not. But in the case of Ethiopia and Mozambique it is an attempt to build socialism by nations that have not passed through the capitalist stage; they are even trying to avoid it. Ethiopia is not, in fact, the first country in which this has happened; Mongolia was the first. My hesitation was caused by whether to call them countries of socialist orientation. They have been trying to become socialist; they aren't socialist yet.

JKG: Let me get you back on track. Let's talk about the development of socialism in the Soviet Union.

SM: There has been tremendous economic progress in all socialist countries. First of all, the Soviet Union has become the second largest industrial power in the world, second only to the United States. I think the socialist countries, taken together, account for about one third of the world's total production.

The next point is that for quite a number of countries socialism has been the road to national sovereignty and independence.

JKG: What do you mean by that?

SM: I mean that some of the socialist countries, like China, have actually gained independence as a result of the socialist transformation. China wasn't exactly a colony before, but it was a semidependent country.

JKG: Yes, we recognize that.

SM: As were Cuba and some other countries. It's important that their movement toward national liberation was combined with the movement toward socialism. Socialism meant the path to their quick economic independence.

JKG: I am going to urge later that in many countries of the world the Soviet influence has been in retreat, as to a considerable extent has ours. The Soviet Union's influence was greater twenty-five years ago in China, North Africa, even Eastern Europe, than it is now.

SM: I am now talking about social systems rather than the influence of any one country. For me, China is just another independent country, not a capitalist one but socialist. It's somewhat different from the Soviet system, and, as everybody knows, it's absolutely independent of the Soviet Union.

It's not a question of our influence or the Chinese influence; it's a question of social organization. In terms of social organization, the Chinese are more or less moving along lines similar to ours.

I think one of the most important advantages that socialism has shown as a system is that it produces a society of social fairness, social justice — a society that tries to bring justice, equality, fairness to all its members.

But let me enumerate some of the other advantages that come with socialism, as I see them. They are the result, first of all, of noncyclical, noncrisis development in the economy, and they come with centralized planning. When central planning is adequately organized, it has the great advantage of being able to redistribute resources in the necessary strategic directions without causing major disruptions in the economy. It's possible to keep the economy moving along an optimal path, which guarantees the fullest and most efficient use of all production resources.

Now that's the ideal, and we see that in many cases we have deviated from that optimal path. But the path is there; the effort is there; and in many ways it's successful. Socialism in the Soviet Union developed at a very fast rate for a number of decades until recently.

I will speak later about the problems of socialism, about the difficulties, the precritical situation as we call it in the Soviet Union, but I want to begin with its successes.

JKG: We all recognize, I think, that in the last seventy years your country has come a long way, economically speaking, from the primitive economy of the Czars.

SM: The advantage of full employment in socialist countries is, as I see it, a great one. Socialism has been able to achieve one of the highest human aspirations: full employment, the elimination of compulsory unemployment. There may be some temporary unemployment under socialism, people changing from one job to another. The number of such people may even be large at any given time, but at least in a socialist society there has been no danger up to now of the abrupt closure of plants or mass layoffs owing to short-term cycles or a long-term structural crisis. That, to me, is a great advantage, but it's a point that is currently being debated in the Soviet Union because some argue that the absence of compulsory unemployment produces a lack of discipline.

JKG: There are still further advantages of socialism you want to mention?

SM: There are, indeed. There is the advantage of social security in the system. There are many services in the Soviet Union that are free or partially free. They are not assured through some kind of market instrument but are guaranteed automatically by the functioning of a socialist state.

JKG: Services such as?

SM: Such as free medical care, free education, pensions on a general scale for everybody, access to recreational facilities, low-cost housing.

JKG: I would say that those are things that the mature capitalist countries have also. Would you agree?

SM: To some extent, yes. There has been movement along those lines.

JKG: You are saying that the welfare state came much more rapidly in the socialist world than in the capitalist, and somewhat more completely?

SM: I think it came more completely, more rapidly, and it came as a general rule rather than as an exception. The welfare state in the United States and Britain is different from the welfare state in the Soviet Union. For example, you don't have free medical services in the United States, or only in certain categories.

JKG: Not completely free, but we will, I hope, move in that direction.

SM: In our country, even though we are much poorer

than you are, these services were established at a very early stage, and they were the result not of abundance but of a conscious effort to achieve a system of social fairness and social justice.

We have also achieved a large measure of social equality. Under socialism there is, in principle, no division between the rich and the poor. This is an important advantage.

JKG: I want to press you on how socialism has changed, not now under Mr. Gorbachev but in the previous seventy years.

SM: Socialism has changed just as capitalism has — socialism and capitalism are in a situation of continual change.

JKG: What would you say were the great changes in the seventy years after Lenin?

SM: The system, as you know, was first established under Lenin, but there was no true socialism then; it was just being started. Socialism really developed after his death, so, in that sense, there was a great change.

JKG: Yes.

SM: Then I mentioned the spread of socialism in the world. That was a big change, for Lenin only lived long enough to see socialism in one country.

JKG: As a distant observer, I want to know more about some of the great changes that occurred inside your country in the years well after the October Revolution. For example, the liquidation of the kulaks.

SM: The liquidation of the kulaks and the collectivization of agriculture. The building of cooperative agriculture was part of the building of socialism in our country.

JKG: But in some ways wasn't this a reversal of the New Economic Policy, the earlier policy under Lenin that had involved some actual liberalization of the system in the 1920s?

SM: Lenin perceived the future of agriculture in the Soviet Union as a cooperative matter, as did others who came after him, but his idea of how to make it cooperative was different from what happened in actual practice. At the end of the 1920s and in the 1930s, under Stalin, collectivization proceeded at such a rapid rate that it brought quite a serious consequence to agriculture. In fact, it led to a stagnation of agricultural production for a period of time and, as you say, to the liquidation in a number of areas of the kulaks — the capitalist farmers who used hired labor — and the liquidation of some people who weren't kulaks at all — well-to-do peasants on what you would call family farms. Now, these people were liquidated in the sense that everybody who didn't want to participate in the collective farms was taken off his land and sent away. That is what happened, but the idea was . . .

JKG: Not the most agreeable.

SM: It was not the most agreeable, but it was done. Collectivization under Stalin proceeded at a forced tempo. Although it was envisaged that rich or well-to-do farmers would participate in and become part of the cooperatives and they would cooperate with socialism and cooperative agriculture, in actual fact they did not, and they were forced to come into the system rather than their coming in voluntarily. Lenin's cooperative plan was implemented but in a way that in many aspects deviated from the way he would have wished.

JKG: I'm not too clear why the tempo had to be so forced, but on another matter: These early years placed particular emphasis, did they not, on heavy industry, and this had an adverse effect on agriculture?

SM: Starting with the late 1920s and the early 1930s, the Soviet Union made a conscious effort to build up heavy industry.

JKG: This was seen as the backbone of socialism?

SM: It was the backbone of the economic independence of the country. The idea was to build a national machine-

building industry, so we wouldn't have to import all kinds
of machinery, machine tools and tractors from abroad. To
have a machine-building industry, you had first to build a
steel industry. And fuel industries. This line of development continued for quite a long time, in fact until the
1950s. It was a conscious effort, and it had to be done at the
expense of agriculture and of light industry — consumer
goods.

JKG: But in the 1950s, there came a greater emphasis on
the consumer goods industry, did there not?

SM: Yes. Starting with 1953, after Stalin died, there was
a deliberate promotion of what we call the second compartment of the economy. The first compartment is heavy
industry; the second compartment is consumer goods. There
was a constant promotion of this by Malenkov and later by
Khrushchev, and also a promotion of agriculture. The idea
was put forth in a theoretical form and then in a more
practical way that consumer goods industries could and should
be developed at a rate that was equal to or even faster than
the rate of development of heavy industry. Previously the
dogma had been that heavy industry should be developed
faster than the consumer goods industry.

JKG: Say a word about Khrushchev and the Soviet economy.

SM: There were many changes under Khrushchev. One
change was in the structure of the economy. He paid a really
great deal of attention to agriculture; under him it started
increasing at a substantial rate. One of his achievements was
opening up the virgin lands in Siberia. This is a point that
is sometimes disputed, but if you look at the overall production of grain in the Soviet Union, a large part of it is
now produced in the virgin lands. That was a positive development under Khrushchev.

The second achievement, I think, was that he turned the
tide in the provision of adequate housing. There was a mass

housing construction program initiated by Khrushchev, which gave families a chance to live in separate apartments for the first time. Previously the rule had been that several families would share the same apartment. When I was a child, our family lived in an apartment that was shared by six families; we had one room in a six-room apartment. That was the rule, and it's no longer the rule. This isn't owing exclusively to Khrushchev, but the big change in that direction started with him.

JKG: I have said on other occasions that, as a visitor to Russia, I always arrive hearing about the terrible housing shortage. Then when I'm there, my impression is of the incredible number of houses that have just been built.

SM: Our present housing shortage is different from that of forty years ago. In a house where I once lived, a small house built in the nineteenth century, we had people living in the basement, one family per room; and, as I explained to you, the apartments were also shared. That was a real shortage. The shortage we have now is that you can't choose between this apartment or that, and many young families aren't able to get their apartments immediately.

JKG: I wasn't being critical.

SM: No, no; I'm not trying to defend.

JKG: You have a further word on Khrushchev?

SM: Khrushchev was naive in many ways. He thought that once the Soviet Union had built this or that number of apartments or produced this or that amount of meat, we would reach an abundance. It turned out that the more you built apartments, the more there was demand for larger apartments on the part of the people. The better off the people got in terms of income, the more the demand developed. So, in that sense, he was naive. He introduced a long paragraph into the charter of the Communist Party of the Soviet Union, stating that the production of this or that amount of meat and the production of this or that amount of housing would mean we would have achieved communism. Now we have to discount that. Still, it was the result of a well-intentioned effort to expand the consumer side of the economy.

There were other changes associated with Khrushchev, but we will talk about them later.

JKG: Why was Khrushchev eased out? Why was he terminated?

SM: He wasn't terminated.

JKG: Why was his term of office brought to an end? I'm trying to use a very mild term. In the United States we might say, why was he sacked, fired?

SM: He was fired basically because he set a limit to his own term of office himself and said he would resign when he reached seventy. When he did reach seventy, he didn't resign, and he went on doing things that weren't extremely popular with the other parts of the leadership, so he had to go.

JKG: You must be more specific. What was unpopular? I don't want to press you unduly.

SM: He was blamed for what was called subjectionism or subjectivity. When he first came, he promoted collective leadership in the Politburo. That meant that all decisions were made on the basis of collective discussion and collective decision-making. As time passed, however, he started making decisions more or less on his own and pressed those decisions on the other members of the Politburo, in some cases without previously consulting with them or without appropriate discussion. People got fed up with that.

One of the decisions, for example, was concerned with separating the party organization into two parts, one that was responsible for agriculture and the other that was responsible for industry, so that in any one region there would be a party committee in charge of agriculture and another in charge of industry. That was a very artificial division and a subjective decision on his part, but, more important, there were many other matters besides agriculture and industry to look after.

JKG: I met Khrushchev when he was in the United States in the late years of the Eisenhower administration. I thought he was a fascinating figure, with a very sharp turn of phrase and a very wide range of information. I have heard it said that he was so widely informed that he got into matters other people thought were their own private property. Is that true?

SM: No; I don't think so. He was a very popular figure in the country. He was also a very shrewd politician and I think in many ways very efficient. In foreign policy he was the first to initiate the policies of détente and the relaxation of relations with the United States. The thaw in our relations around the late 1950s was due to Khrushchev, and my father, who was ambassador at the time, was specifically sent to Washington to help achieve that change. In many ways we did manage a kind of détente until the unfortunate incident with the U-2 in 1960, which turned the tide for a number of years.

In economics he did a lot, as I've said, but, especially in his later years, he started to make decisions that weren't really substantiated and I think that is what . . .

JKG: That is what I was trying to say. He got into matters on which he wasn't fully informed.

SM: It wasn't a question of information, I think. He had wrong ideas about how to manage certain things, and he started to press those wrong ideas on others, and they didn't agree with him.

JKG: Now, what do you see as the further developments in recent times that led to the need for the Gorbachev reforms?

SM: That's what I wanted to talk about. I have said previously that socialism has gained a lot, but there are many things we thought we would gain, we would accomplish, that we didn't gain or accomplish. Lenin's idea was that socialism could successfully compete with capitalism only if it reached higher productivity, higher labor productivity, higher economic productivity in general. Now it has to be said that socialism has not achieved the highest productivity in the world; it's still inferior to the most developed industrial capitalist countries in that respect.

Lenin's idea also was that socialism would bring about the highest living standards in the world, and we haven't achieved those either. There were various reasons for that. There was the Second World War, but more than forty years have passed since then, and we have had examples of countries that have changed completely in that time. Japan has achieved enormous economic results and living standards very close to those in the United States. Meanwhile we in the Soviet Union have lagged behind. I think to a large extent it is due to a deceleration of economic growth during the last ten or fifteen years in the Soviet economy. But not only in our economy, in the economies of some of the other socialist countries as well. In the beginning of the 1970s, our gross national product was still growing at a rate of about five or six percent per annum, but by the end of the seventies and especially in the beginning of the eighties, we had come down to between one and three percent at the maximum. This was absolutely inadequate, but the important thing is that it was a long-term deceleration, a long-term slowdown. There was also a long-term slowdown in the capitalist world, but we will talk later about the different reasons for that. In the socialist world the deceleration still continues today; we still haven't turned the tide.

This slowdown was already starting to occur in the middle of the 1970s, and by the end of that decade it was recognized by most economists and politicians in the Soviet Union. Brezhnev, who was General Secretary at the time, talked about it and the necessity of overcoming it. And it also became a serious problem for the socialist countries in Eastern Europe. It occurred partially as the result of an increase in fuel prices, but it was also a more general phenomenon, and it led to what is now called a period of new revolutionary reforms.

JKG: Let me ask one further question, which reflects an old interest of mine. During all of this period, in spite of some improvements and the use of the virgin lands, agriculture in the Soviet Union has remained a difficult problem, has it not? One evidence of that is the very large imports of grain by a country that once was called the breadbasket of Europe. What is your view of the agriculture problem in your country?

SM: Well, Khrushchev had the idea that agriculture could be developed without large capital investment by developing the virgin lands, by raising prices for farm products and by making the collective farmers a little bit freer to decide what to plant and so on. Basically, however, he wanted to achieve greater agricultural production without relying on large capital investment. This, I think, was a great mistake, and, under Brezhnev, it changed. A large part of our resources went into capital investment in agriculture. Prices for agricultural commodities were increased again, and the system was liberalized to some extent. But even so, substantial results have not been achieved. Capital investment in agriculture still tends to be inefficient in most cases; I think the basic reason is the same as for the deceleration or slowdown of the economy as a whole — the bureaucratic mismanagement of the industry.

JKG: I have, by all available Soviet standards, a deeply reactionary thought. It is that agriculture around the world and over the centuries has really worked well only when it has been under the direction of the owner-manager. He exploits himself and his family rather than being subject to a larger productive apparatus. You notice I use the word "exploit." I don't deny for a moment that an individual forces himself to work very hard — harder than he can be forced to work by a boss. Do you agree with that?

sm: I agree, but I also disagree. The reason I disagree is not based on any communist or socialist dogma. First, as to private agriculture, it has been successful in some areas and not very successful in others. Take Poland, for example. Polish agriculture is private, mostly private, and it isn't tremendously successful. I am not criticizing Poland; I am stating it as a fact. Now, the owner-operator farming, say, in the United States has been successful. But he is successful because his farm is part of what we call agroindustry. It may be organized on an individual or autonomous basis, but it's part of the agrobusiness industry. I think this is a fact that is recognized by most people in your country. Industry has served your agriculture well, and not just industry but also various other services, like banking. Basically we are now trying to do the same thing in the Soviet Union. We even have a ministry for agrobusiness. The question is, however, whether agrobusiness can be run by a form of ministerial organization or a set of organizations that don't produce anything but whose task is one of coordination. Or must agriculture and industry be integrated at the level of production, as is now the case in Canada or the United States?

jkg: I think I see your point, but do elaborate.

sm: The point is that the less there is interference with those people who really produce and organize the production of things, whether it is in agriculture or in industry that serves agriculture, the better things work. However, the idea of a family farmer by himself toiling on his own soil surrounded by nature is archaic in the world of modern technology.

JKG: Tomorrow let's talk about the problems of the Soviet economy and then go on later to the Gorbachev reforms and the prospects for socialism. Then we can return to capitalism and its problems and prospects and to coexistence between the two systems. How does that sound?

SM: That's fine.

2

Socialism Now:
The Causes of the Slowdown

JKG: You have made an impressive case for the accomplishments of socialism in the half century or so following the Revolution. I am prepared to believe that economic life was a good deal more ample then than under the Czars. Now, however, let us speak of the slowdown in recent times. How has this occurred? What are the causes?

SM: The slowdown started in the latter part of the 1970s and was particularly significant in the early 1980s. As I said in our earlier conversation, the basic figures are that until that time — and I'm referring to the Soviet experience now, not to that of other socialist countries — our gross national product had been expanding at an annual rate of about five or six percent, whereas by the beginning of the 1980s, it went down to around two or three percent.

JKG: Ours went down very sharply during those years too. You didn't have Professor Milton Friedman and our experiment with tough monetarism, did you?

SM: No, we didn't. I believe there are some similarities in the causes of our slowdowns, but there are also differences.

JKG: I wasn't to be taken seriously on that.

sm: Maybe Professor Friedman did lend a hand somewhere from the American Embassy or through the American Embassy; I don't really know.

As to the figures, two or three percent may seem to be quite a respectable rate of growth for the United Kingdom or even for the United States, but in Russia it was felt that this was tantamount to stagnation; and, in fact, that is how Mr. Gorbachev is describing the situation right now. It is really a serious thing; let me go into the causes of it.

jkg: What would you say was the most important cause?

sm: Maybe I should start with the least important. Perhaps the least important cause was something shared by capitalism and socialism, and that was the steep rise in the cost of energy in the middle of the 1970s. Socialism was fairly slow to adjust to the high cost of oil.

jkg: To what we called the oil shock?

sm: Well, yes, the oil shock. There was a steep rise in fuel prices, not just oil but also gas and coal, and this brought about an economic slowdown, particularly in the countries of Eastern Europe.

The Soviet Union is a producer and exporter of oil, so it wasn't hurt, but by the beginning of the 1980s, we had hit a physical limit to its production. The increase in the production of oil stopped, and we reached a plateau.

I think in the capitalist world the causes of the oil shock were different. You didn't hit a physical limit, but you were affected by the sharp rise in oil prices. In our case, there was a limit on what we could produce, and that was what chiefly affected our economy.

jkg: We had more oil at a higher cost, and you had the same cost but less oil or no increase.

sm: No increase, and for some Eastern European countries, in fact, there was a decrease because we had to use more oil in our own country and could export less.

jkg: So much for oil. In those days we had quite a few

economists who wanted to blame all their own shortcomings as to policy on the Arabs. We must both be careful not to do that!

sm: In this case we had only ourselves to blame because we were producing the oil, not buying it. *You* could blame the shortage on the Arabs; we had to blame ourselves.

jkg: What are the other reasons for the slowdown?

sm: Another factor besides the rise in energy costs was that it became exceedingly difficult to export to the West because of the stagnation in the American and other Western markets. This led to a lot of problems and particularly to the deterioration in our trade balances. In many cases, they became negative, and the foreign indebtedness of the Soviet Union and of some of the other socialist countries increased enormously, sometimes even making it necessary to cut imports. This aggravated the generally unfavorable economic situation because imports are a substantial productive input into our economies.

jkg: And, as in Poland, there was already a very heavy debt structure?

sm: Yes. And Romania was hurt because in the preceding years it had managed to become a substantial producer of a number of industrial goods, including supertankers, but by the time it could produce them, the market had fallen and it couldn't sell them.

jkg: This was an overflow onto the socialist world from the difficulties in the capitalist world?

sm: Exactly, but the main reasons for our economic slowdown were, I think, internal, and I think most people would share my view.

jkg: What were the internal reasons?

sm: Some people believe that the so-called Kondratiev cycle — a long wave in economic activity that is self-generating — affected the capitalist and socialist worlds more or less at the same time. We in the socialist world are held to be in a kind of a Kondratiev cycle right now in our internal operations.

Now, I know you don't believe in the Kondratiev cycle, but I believe in it for the capitalist world. In the socialist world the situation is totally different, and I don't think the Kondratiev cycle is appropriate.

Nonetheless, we are having a slowdown now, and it is occurring at the same time as one in the capitalist world, but let us look at the differences. While capitalism was struck by mass unemployment in the seventies and eighties, socialism was encountering an increasing shortfall of manpower. While the Western countries were experiencing large unused production capacities, particularly in a number of basic industries such as steel, machine tools and the like, the socialist economies were finding it difficult to increase their capacities at the rate necessary to maintain their traditional growth rates. So, all together, the nature of the economic problem in the two societies seems to be quite different.

JKG: We had an excess of production, and you had a shortage of production.

SM: We had a shortage of production, and we weren't able to overcome it.

JKG: We want to talk again about your shortage of labor. Is it a shortage of people willing and able to do hard manual work?

SM: It isn't that there aren't enough manual laborers; there is a general lack of manpower.

Perhaps I should put it this way: somewhere in the 1970s the socialist economies and particularly the Soviet Union came to a turning point in their overall economic conditions. Before that, we had had what I would call plentiful resources of labor, most of the necessary raw materials and a good supply of oil and the other fuels. But somewhere in the seventies, we bumped into a situation where there was suddenly not enough of all those factors of production.

JKG: I don't want to interrupt the discussion here, but we would have had such a shortage of labor in the United States, particularly for less prestigious work, if we hadn't had the Mexicans, the West Indians and others from abroad. You wouldn't want to consider allowing in the Chinese and the Indians to relieve your labor shortages, I take it?

SM: That question did arise once. It was sometime in the mid-1950s, when the Chinese suggested that they provide us with their excess labor. This was considered, but it wasn't approved of as a practical solution. At that time — it was under Khrushchev — a shortage of labor was not yet a problem in our country. In the fifties and early sixties, you see, we had an ample supply of manpower that came from the villages, away from agriculture. We had a continuous flow of labor from the country to the cities, a flow particularly of young people, of men who had gone through the armed services, who didn't want to go back to agriculture and who ended up in the industrial enterprises instead. So the industrial enterprises had no difficulty recruiting manpower at that time. There were, as well, a substantial number of women leaving the agricultural area and seeking employment in the cities.

With that kind of labor flow, the industrial enterprises didn't really have to think about economizing on labor costs or looking in any real way for a new source of manpower; they had workers waiting at their doorsteps. I don't mean there was unemployment. No, these people just came in, and there were jobs for them immediately; the jobs were there.

JKG: I want to press you on to some other things. There has been much talk, some of it in our earlier conversation, about the specific inefficiencies of the Soviet economy. Can you talk a little bit about that?

SM: Yes. As I've said, this plentiful supply of labor changed in the seventies and eventually dried up. In those earlier years, we had ninety-two percent of all able-bodied adult men and women working and employed effectively. Now there came a deficit situation in the labor supply. At the same time we came to use the labor that was employed less effectively. The efficiency of our workers was not as high as we would have liked it to be; even by our standards, it was low.

Many plants accumulated excess workers whom they paid, but they held them in reserve and used them only when they were needed, and particularly when it was desirable to increase output suddenly at the end of a planning period.

JKG: Labor was stockpiled?

SM: Exactly. Labor was stockpiled, and it was generally used inefficiently. For a large part of a month, for example, or of a quarter or of a year it wouldn't be used to its full capacity.

JKG: What about capital growth? Were capital goods stockpiled as well?

SM: No, not exactly. We have always had a deficit of capital goods in the Soviet Union. The share of gross national product used for capital investment in the fifties and sixties was very large, maybe not as large as in Japan, but quite large — as much as thirty-five percent. In Japan it was forty percent. These are very high figures. This made it possible to maintain construction of a great number of industrial enterprises all around the country. If you were in the Soviet Union in those years, you probably saw the vast construction. Everywhere you went, there was construction, construction and more construction. A lot of funds were used for that and for setting up new electric power stations, mining facilities and so on.

JKG: I have heard it said, most recently in a paper from the Soviet Union that I was reading yesterday, that this was a period when there was far too much emphasis on building new plants and far too little on improving and adapting the capital equipment in the existing ones. Is that your view?

SM: That is true; I will go on to it just a bit later. I would like to say first that, starting with the Khrushchev period, real wages started increasing. There was a conscious effort to increase the social payments, the wages of lower-paid labor. Real incomes increased.

But because they increased rapidly, the share of the gross national product that could be used for capital investment became smaller, so, step by step, we got ourselves into a situation where we had less of what we produced available for capital investment. The share for consumption went up, and the share for capital investment went down, and there was an even larger deficit of capital goods.

JKG: Here again there are strong overtones of the West. There are several thousand economists in the United States who wake up every morning and say that we must have more savings and less consumption. What you are saying has a very familiar ring.

SM: We were proceeding from a rather low wage level to a higher wage level, and people were spending enormously. I remember maybe thirty years ago there were things that were in ample supply. For example, you could buy caviar anywhere at a fairly low price. People weren't in the market for caviar. Now, when wages rose in the sixties and seventies, there wasn't enough caviar to export or even to sell in local markets.

JKG: Let's go on to some of the other things that went wrong.

SM: Yesterday I mentioned Khrushchev's housing program. That took a lot of additional resources from capital investment into construction, which was a minus for capital investment. As we observed earlier, the Soviet Union built its industrial potential in the thirties, the late forties and the fifties. By the beginning of the eighties, all this needed substantial reconstruction; even the equipment installed in the fifties and sixties was nearing the end of its physical life cycle. Now the supply of capital goods and investment funds was simply inadequate to cover these additional requirements. So, although there was construction of new plants going on, there was a serious problem trying to maintain existing production capacity, let alone creating new capacity.

JKG: In some sense, new plants were created at the expense of the modernization of the old ones.

SM: Exactly, but not just modernization. In some cases there wasn't enough maintenance of old plants, so they became exceedingly outmoded, outdated, and occasionally they were even physically destroyed. This added to the deficit situation.

JKG: Let me press you on some other matters of which I have read. What is the meaning of the reference to the crisis in agriculture in these years?

SM: I think that the crisis in agriculture was something that aggravated the overall situation because we had to spend hard currency that had been earned from our oil exports for buying grain instead of using it to import more of the machinery that was necessary to modernize our industry. That didn't occur according to the plan but because agriculture reached a limit beyond which it didn't expand its production. It expanded up until the late seventies, and then it stopped.

JKG: Why did it stop?

SM: I think we reached some kind of physical limit beyond which it wasn't possible to go with the old system of centralized management of agriculture. Agriculture had been managed by central authorities and by local authorities. The farmers didn't really decide what to produce, and they had to put up with everyday interference in their activities. This may have been a good way to expand production in the virgin lands, where there was production for the first time, and to bring people into the operations. It was not a good system for improving the productivity of the established crop-bearing and animal-breeding agriculture.

JKG: You are saying that the Soviet farmers needed more market incentives, more of the spur of capitalist self-interest?

SM: I think what they needed was more possibility to work and to come to their own decisions. They needed less interference from people who didn't understand the local specifics of the land or how to operate in the particular region, who set plans and norms that might be correct for the country as a whole but that weren't right for the specific region involved.

Recently I read a good article about agriculture in Estonia, which compared it with agriculture in a region of the neighboring Russian republic. It's the same socialist system, but the Estonians are much more productive. There is less interference in Estonia and more interference in the Russian republic. The Estonians like to say, "We prefer to use our own foolish heads instead of somebody's wise head thinking for us."

JKG: Also you are getting close to saying that agriculture works best when the individual makes his own decisions and gets his own return.

SM: What I am saying is that the individual collective farm should be free to make its own decisions. That doesn't necessarily mean that individual private farmers should be.

JKG: You are still sticking with the collective farm?

SM: We are still sticking with the collective farm and the state farm. We believe in a system of personal and family incentives inside the collective farm, and also in more incentives for farmers operating on their own private plots. This system can produce good results without continuous interference from outside. We will talk about it later when we talk about the current reforms.

Now, just to reiterate, we got into a situation where we had to import more grain, including, very importantly, feed grain for the cattle.

JKG: Which we love to have you buy.

SM: Which you love to have us buy, and our people love to eat more meat and less bread. They are all staples, so to say, but the cattle have to be fed if we are to have beef. Thus there was a demand for feed grain, and after a while this had to be imported from the West in place of the machinery that was needed for the modernization of industry. That led to a stagnation in industry and to a situation where we were really exchanging very precious fuel for feed grain, which robbed us of the possibility of modernizing as fast as we wanted to.

JKG: You were subsidizing our farm bloc rather than our machine-tool industry?

SM: That's true.

JKG: But what about reform? I have heard you say that some of the reforms that are needed go to the very foundation of the socialist system.

SM: I would say that by the end of what is called the Brezhnev period — a long period starting in 1964 and ending in 1984 — the stage was set for a drastic reappraisal of the "precrisis situation," as Mr. Gorbachev calls it. The current discussion in the Soviet Union of the causes and solutions to this precrisis is essential to understanding the future of our society in the coming decades.

This discussion is also important because it goes beyond the immediate problems we have just been mentioning, beyond the immediate difficulties. It questions the existing manner in which we are operating a socialist country. We will go into it all in our next conversation.

3

Socialism Now:
The Causes of the Slowdown

(Continued)

JKG: Now let's talk about what led specifically to the Gorbachev reforms. Why such a drastic change — what I have heard you call a revolution?

SM: For the first time since the Soviet Union was established, it has been replacing the very foundations of socialist society. Not only of the economy but also in the social and political spheres. So the question is asked continuously in our country, why were we so slow to adjust? Everybody realizes the problems were already there in the Brezhnev period. We constantly talked about labor, the supply of capital goods, fuel and so on. Why then did it take us so long to change?

Practically everybody agrees that the main culprit in the economic slowdown and stagnation was the existing system of planning and managing the economy. The system was overcentralized; the central authorities were attempting to relate to, and interfere in, practically every detail of economic life. This led to enterprises having very little, if any, incentive; very little, if any, possibility of solving their own problems.

JKG: Individual incentive had been replaced by bureaucratic supervision?

SM: Exactly. The enterprises were increasingly uninterested in higher efficiency, faster technical progress. There were bureaucratic commands from the top all the way down to the actual production from people who didn't involve themselves in or understand the work being done. This had become the prevalent style and method of operating the economy; and this, I want to reiterate, was particularly detrimental to agriculture. I agree completely with you in that respect. In agriculture it wasn't only the central authorities that interfered but also the local authorities.

JKG: I have heard all this referred to as a system of bureaucratic control and bureaucratic command. Is that true?

SM: That's right, we use those expressions. Yes, the bureaucracy did command. And the important thing is that while it gave the command, it bore no responsibility for the result of the command.

JKG: That was a pleasant situation for those in control; they had the power without the responsibility.

SM: The power without the responsibility, exactly, and that is exactly what people are saying now in our country. This was also true not only in agriculture but in the industrial enterprises. Profits were taken away from the efficient enterprises and used to support the inefficient ones. The efficient enterprises didn't really have any incentive to work better; it wasn't possible for them to use their profits or their depreciation funds to improve their conditions. The depreciation funds were taken away from them, so they couldn't even replace the machinery. That was one of the reasons we became somewhat backward in technical progress as compared to the leading capitalist countries.

JKG: I want to ask one question that obviously arises here. The system did produce a lot of results. But given its deficiencies, why did it operate at all?

s m: People do ask that, and you put it more or less diplomatically. When the system was established sometime in the 1930s, it became a very effective tool of rapid economic growth. In a few decades, as we've noted, it made the Soviet Union the second largest industrial, and for that matter military, power in the world. The country became the largest producer of steel, of oil, even of shoes, and of a number of other industrial products. The trouble, though, was that after a certain time there was a very definite change because the country, which had never had a large industrial potential, now had one. However, there weren't enough of the specific kinds of steel necessary to produce new kinds of goods. There were plenty of low-quality shoes, but the consumers didn't want to buy them. They preferred imported stuff, which was more fashionable and better and higher in quality.

j k g: That's a point to which I want to return.

s m: Right. Industry was also late in producing main-frame computers, personal computers and microcomputers.

j k g: You were slow in going from technological achievement to actual use?

s m: Exactly. Video cassette recorders, many other consumer novelties — we were always backward. This isn't something specific to the Soviet Union or to the Russian or Slavic nature. You look at all socialist countries; they are backward in that specific area — in producing the things that are needed at the time they are needed, even though there is the production potential to do so. That is, I think, the core of the problem. They're also late in producing new technology, while the economy is starving for it. Socialism, however, is a good system to build up a large industrial potential quickly. I think that is why quite a number of countries pursued the socialist path and chose that path, especially those that were economically underdeveloped. They saw a way to develop fast.

JKG: With some encouragement from the Soviet Union.

SM: Well, yes and no. We couldn't really encourage them. We did encourage Cuba and we assisted the Cubans, but they made the choice to become socialist. I won't talk here about Eastern Europe, where you can say we helped them by the use of force, which isn't exactly true, but China chose socialism.

JKG: Yes, I quite agree.

SM: And Vietnam and the African socialist-oriented countries.

JKG: Perhaps we could say, in a mild way, that you had a certain encouraging role in Eastern Europe?

SM: Yes. The important thing is, however, that you shouldn't underestimate the capacity of a centralized economy to develop an industrial base quickly. I think that that's important. It can develop the industrial base, but the question then is whether it can operate it efficiently, and I'm afraid it has been proved that an overcentralized society cannot do so. This was first realized in the late 1950s in our country.

JKG: As early as that?

SM: Yes, thirty years ago.

JKG: This is interesting to me because I heard discussions along this line in 1959, when I was there.

SM: I was a young man at that time, and I remember the problem was already obvious then. There was a discussion in the late fifties, when Khrushchev and other leaders of our country said that the system was overcentralized and too complex, much too complex to plan and operate from a single headquarters. This was said exactly in those words. There is nothing new in that.

And in 1958, under Khrushchev, the centralized ministries were, in fact, discontinued. They had been set up under Stalin in the early 1930s, and they mushroomed in the early fifties after the war. When they were discontinued, the administration of all enterprises was moved from Moscow to the Regional Economic Councils.

JKG: What was their Russian name?

SM: The *sovnarkhozes*.

JKG: They were much discussed when I was there in 1959.

SM: Yes, they had originally been in existence in the twenties, before the ministries were set up. This was Khrushchev's idea: to go back to Lenin's way of operating the economy, to go from overcentralization to the more regionally dispersed operation of the *sovnarkhozes*.

It was the first substantial conscious effort to decentralize on a general scale. That, as I say, was in the late fifties. Then in the early sixties, Eusey Lieberman, the economist from Kharkov, first stated that the economy of the Soviet Union, the socialist economy, could be operated on the basis of profit. This was a revelation to the world, and people said socialism was moving toward capitalism.

JKG: I once encountered Lieberman when I was giving some lectures in Italy. I recall how greatly impressed I was at hearing that the Soviet Union was returning to the profit system.

SM: This was also under Khrushchev, and the economic discussion started in the early sixties. The general slogan at that time, exactly as it is now, was economic freedom for the enterprises, thus putting the profit motive at the center of planning and management. This led to reforms in 1964 and '65 in both industry and agriculture, and these reforms were implemented under Brezhnev and Kosygin, the new leadership that came in at that time. The reforms formally spelled out the right of the enterprises to use part of their profits for capital investment, for investment in the social sphere and for bonuses to workers. It all sounded right, but the ministries were being reestablished at the same time. In other words, the reforms gave freedom to the enterprises and at the same time provided for the reestablishment of the ministries.

The ministries were thought, exactly as they are thought now, to be strategic agencies that would develop and help pursue technical progress and assist the enterprises financially when and if necessary. They were not to interfere with the daily management of the plants, and this was carefully spelled out, as it is spelled out now. In a sense, we are returning to what we wanted to do then. The ministries were not supposed to interfere, but, in actual fact, within the next ten years they took over the day-to-day management and fully reestablished themselves as the overcentralized leaders of industry.

JKG: I have some questions.

SM: Okay. There were some reforms in agriculture, but I will come to those later.

JKG: My first question after this very interesting overview of history is the obvious one. It could have some relevance to the capitalist world of the United States. Are you saying that there is a certain inevitability about centralization? You have had repeated efforts to deal with it; it has always come back. Doesn't this derive from the desire of the ministry or the bureaucrat for power? And from the fact that the latter says to himself, "Well, it's my responsibility. If anything goes wrong, I will be blamed, so therefore I must be in control"?

What I am asking is this: Aren't you contending here with a process of extraordinary power? This becomes particularly interesting when we talk about the problems Mr. Gorbachev now faces.

SM: I think you have put your finger on one of the many problems of our time. It's true that both of our systems have seen a rise in the power of the bureaucracy; we will come

to that in our later discussions. We will bump into bureaucracy all the way through, in the economic and the cultural,
the military and the political spheres.

JKG: And the tendency for bureaucratic centralization —

SM: And we will come to the problem of bureaucratic
centralization.

JKG: Which is one of the fundamental tendencies of our
time?

SM: Yes. But let me return to the case of agriculture,
where Mr. Brezhnev is blamed for all its centralization. In
fact, the first thing he did in agriculture was to promote a
reform that was in exactly the opposite direction. It was in
his speech to the plenary session of the Central Committee
in March 1965. He said collective farms were to be given
the right to sell freely in the market whatever they produced
in excess of their quotas. Farmers were paid money for their
work for the first time instead of being paid in kind for the
work they did on the collective farms. Farmers now started
getting pensions; older farmers for the first time had social
security, old-age pensions; large capital investment funds
were channeled to agriculture. But in actual fact and not
just in words, the system of day-to-day interference in the
management of the farms continued. This led to stagnation
of output and made the economic incentives envisaged by
the Brezhnev reforms ineffective.

JKG: Let me ask you a second question about something
you haven't mentioned, which has impressed me. That is
the problem of socialism in the consumer goods economy.
In the age of Lenin or Stalin, the economic system produced
a few very simple goods — steel, machinery, some other capital goods, elementary food, clothing, fuel and shelter. Not
much else. Under these circumstances, anyone can see what
the input-output relationships are. The problem of planning
is readily perceived. But now, seventy years after the Revo-

lution, an enormous range of consumer goods is possible, and within that range of goods there are different styles, different designs, different service and repair requirements. This supply of consumer goods in all its variety is the norm; this is the standard in Western Europe and the United States. Doesn't that impose a particularly difficult burden on centralized socialist planning?

sM: I think you are essentially right in pointing to the differences between the modern economy and the economy of the 1920s and 1930s. It is true that the number and variety of goods produced are very different now from what they were in those times. However, I don't think that, in principle, the problem of solving the input-output relationships in modern times is impossible. I think it's mathematically possible.

jKG: Can you take the computer printouts and put them into action? That's a different question.

sM: There are transnational corporations that are doing it all over the world and doing it fairly well. And the United States has large corporations that are pretty centralized.

jKG: But they are surrounded by small service enterprises. And while the Ford Motor Company or General Motors can and does produce the cars, it doesn't service them itself.

sM: The important thing is to find a good balance between what has to be done by the central management of those large corporations or, for that matter, by large ministries and central planning authorities in the socialist countries, and what has to be done at the lower levels. There has to be a clear division there.

jKG: This has to be done in response to the market?

sM: In response to the market, yes; that is one of the meanings of the Gorbachev reforms.

jKG: Let me go on to another problem that has impressed me on my brief passages through the Soviet Union, and that

is inflation. One is told that the price of bread hasn't changed
since 1947.

sm: It has changed recently.

jkg: And there are many other things that have been
intensely stable as to price.

sm: Housing, for example.

jkg: Yes. But in the Soviet Union one sees long lines
waiting to get into the stores, which is the Soviet form of
inflation. There is more money than there are goods. The
officials of your state bank once told me that the system was
under great political pressure always to provide more income than there were things to buy. Isn't that a tendency
in your country and in the socialist economy in general?

sm: You see, in principle, the planning authorities are
expected to balance demand and supply when they set up
a national plan. Then they break the national plan down
into plans for various commodities and so on. It is an essential requirement that they achieve a balance before the
plan is adopted, and they do it, but they do it on a theoretical
basis. They set up a production plan that is equal to fore-
casted demand, but then they don't give the enterprises sufficient resources to implement it. The enterprises then try
to fulfill their quotas by producing whatever they can, but
that production isn't necessarily geared to the specific products that are in demand. Things are produced that are not
needed, and at the same time things that are needed by the
population are not produced.

jkg: High boots might be made but not good women's
shoes?

sm: The enterprises will produce shoes, but it won't be
the kind of shoes the population needs. Why is this so? It's
not because they are stupid but because, for example, they
have a quota saying they must produce this or that number
of shoes. That quota is broken down into the categories that

are needed by the population, but the enterprises aren't given enough resources to do it right.

JKG: You are saying that this produces lines at the stores?

SM: I think it is one reason for the hidden inflation, the slow inflation you were talking about. There are other reasons.

JKG: The people at the state bank said that in any reform in the Soviet Union wages would be increased for lower-paid and less prestigious workers and to encourage increased productivity. All of this has a tendency to make incomes exceed the supply of goods — what I have called the Soviet form of inflation.

SM: There is no one simple explanation for what is wrong. I gave you one; the state bank officials gave you another. What they were saying is that the plants aren't interested in economizing on labor or costs. In principle, the plan is to balance the wage bill with the amount of goods that can be sold for those wages. In actual fact, the total wage bill is continuously out of balance. The actual wages paid to the workers are larger than the plan calls for. Why is this so? Because the enterprises aren't interested in saving on labor, and so they overpay and overhire. They pay more than they are supposed to pay because they want to get the workers to produce more.

JKG: I think we have covered the problems of socialism except perhaps for a few more words on the problem of bureaucracy. Do you have something you want to add on that?

SM: There is quite a lot to be said about bureaucracy. I think that the reason we were so slow in changing the overcentralization of planning and management is that it has brought into existence a social stratum of bureaucracy, a bureaucracy that has a vested interest in preserving itself. Maybe we can talk later on about the different kinds of bureaucracy and the psychological reasons why a man wants to wield power. But when you have an overcentralized system, you inevitably have a significant social stratum that is centrally managing the economy. Now, this stratum in the Soviet Union is composed of a growing number of high- and medium-level government employees in the economic ministries, the economic agencies having to do with the planning and distribution of goods.

JKG: They consider themselves pretty well paid, do they?

SM: Some of them are fairly well paid. Others get less, but the important thing is that they feel they are very stable in their positions, and, in addition to payment, they also have social prestige.

JKG: Power?

SM: Sometimes the position by itself doesn't have any power vested in it, but in a deficit economy you can use your position to give yourself power.

JKG: Go ahead, because the dynamics of bureaucracy interest me very much.

SM: Mr. Gorbachev says that at the present time we have eighteen million people out of a population of two hundred eighty million — fifteen percent of the total labor force — in that stratum of bureaucracy. Not all of them are bureaucrats, but they are working in management and in various positions of management and administration. It's far too high a percentage for any society.

This bureaucracy mushroomed after 1964, after the reforms that were meant to liquidate centralization. The ministries were reestablished, and people were returned from the *sovnarkhozes*. They started to enlarge and strengthen the mechanism, trying to ensure that it became permanent and indestructible. They worked to make it indispensable in the public eye, in their own eyes and in the common ideology.

In fact, Khrushchev was criticized by some for creating *sovnarkhozes* and destroying the ministries. He was accused of destroying central planning and undermining socialism.

This, of course, was not the case because central planning isn't identical with the existence of the ministries. The latter have no monopoly on central planning.

The principal function of central planning is different from the supervisory role of the ministries. It is meant to forecast, to foresee the overall development of the economy, to predetermine the overall proportions between supply and demand. Also to pursue a certain policy on capital investment, on social development, on defense and other priorities. Central planning is meant to give the means to channel the resources as necessary according to the total economic strategy of the country and to be able to control the implementation of the plan.

However, as time went on, most of the work that was actually performed by the central planning authorities and the ministries had nothing to do with either forecasting or general strategy. Nor did it have anything to do with maintaining the overall balance between income and supply of which you were speaking. The everyday activity concentrated on rationing and allocation of resources, including current output. In other words, the central agencies and the ministries became something of a substitute for the normal market mechanism. They wanted to take over the things that were done by the market in the capitalist system — the direct buying and selling of commodities between enterprises. It is clear that if the enterprises are in a position to buy whatever they need or sell whatever they make beyond their government contracts at their own will and discretion, there is no need for them to apply to ministries or to anybody else. So here is the problem. The bureaucracy, the centralized bureaucracy — those eighteen million people — were not doing what they were supposed to do under the principles of socialism. They were trying to substitute for the market, trying to work instead of the market, and they couldn't do it. It just wasn't possible, however well meaning they might have been.

JKG: I have heard it said by you and many others that bureaucracy is in some ways a response to a deficit economy or an economy that isn't providing as many goods and services as people want. Is that true?

SM: Yes. I have been describing a system of central allocation of everything by the bureaucracy, which is a system of rationing everything, and the excuse for doing that is the existence of deficits or inadequate supply. Because there isn't enough of anything, goods can't be distributed through the market; they have to be centrally allocated. To do this, you need people of a certain kind who don't produce the things but keep giving them out, distributing them.

JKG: The allocation or rationing then is, to some extent, a function of the excess of demand for goods and services that we were talking about a moment ago?

SM: Yes, but the important thing is that this kind of system tends to re-create or reproduce deficit conditions. By killing incentives, it is continuously reproducing and reestablishing conditions of inadequate supply and abundant demand. Even superabundant demand.

In other words, bureaucracy — an economic bureaucracy like the one I've described — and inadequate resources come together; they feed each other. Bureaucracy feeds inadequate supply and inadequate supply feeds bureaucracy.

JKG: Let me ask a question about the culture of bureaucracy, a question that grows out of my own observation here in the United States: in a great organization, including the great corporate organization, there is a strong tendency to measure superior intelligence by its resemblance to what is already being done and to measure the intelligence of the people who are being added to the organization or who are being promoted by its resemblance to that of the people who are already there or the people who are doing the promoting. Is that your observation in the Soviet Union?

SM: That is absolutely true. Bureaucracy is more or less a corporate kind of system that operates in the same way in different countries, whether it's in a capitalist or a socialist society. It's a bit different under capitalism than under socialism, but it does incline to certain specifics under both. We needn't assume that bureaucracy is essentially evil; it's just that people can't work effectively in certain conditions. Let's imagine ourselves in the position of somebody who is operating within a ministry. He has a number of plants under his control, and he gets certain instructions from the top command to produce a specific product. Now, he hasn't got resources adequate to do so. Those resources are under different ministries or in plants in other ministries, and those ministries or plants are in no position to receive orders from him. The only people he can give orders to are the people under him. So he gives orders to his plant managers to produce something that is not specified by the plan but that can implement the order of the higher authority. He wants the plant managers to do exactly what he says. Under these conditions, a plant manager will not be operating in the interest of his enterprise or to promote its efficiency.

JKG: He is operating in the interest of his superiors?

SM: Yes, and the superiors will always try to put in as managers of the enterprises people who are ready to do as they are told. So, even though, in theory, the plant managers seem to be interested in the profit motive and productive efficiency, they will still be people who will be, as we say in the Soviet Union, looking into the mouths of their superiors.

JKG: Let's get back to something we were talking about earlier, the dynamics of bureaucracy. This superior, this man in the ministry, says to himself, "I am, after all, responsible, and I am the man whose head gets cut off if there aren't results." Accordingly, will he not always be taking power to himself, authority to himself, as a measure of self-protection?

sм: Yes, of course he will. Suppose, for example, the steel industry doesn't produce steel as planned by the central authority. Who is going to be taken to task? At first it will be the people in the ministries, not those on the producing level, and the ministries will then take to task the people who produce.

jкg: So the people in the ministries are going to hold on to authority against the day when they are taken to task?

sм: Right.

jкg: Let me ask you a question about another deficiency of which I have heard mention and which we haven't talked about. When the economy is operating under conditions of inadequate supply, a shadow economy appears, does it not? When the economy doesn't provide certain services, car repairs, for example, then people come along outside the system to repair cars for pay. How do you see the shadow economy? Tell me about it.

sм: Deficit conditions and allocation by rationing and not by price are favorable for breeding corruption, black market operations and a shadow economy, and there's no way they can be eliminated. All of them, unfortunately, have become essential features of the Soviet economy, and particularly since the late 1960s.

jкg: Why did these conditions start then?

sм: They actually didn't start then, but that's when they expanded. As bureaucracy expanded, deficit conditions became more rigid. And conditions of undersupply spread to all parts of the economy. This created a mass movement toward a shadow economy.

jкg: Didn't a shadow economy also come about because there was a need for consumer goods and more services, and because the planning system was increasingly incapable of supplying exactly what the consumer wanted?

SM: Partly that's true, but I must say that the shadow economy sometimes has nothing to do with the consumer. I will give you an example. I don't know whether you know about the so-called cotton bonanza in Uzbekistan. Have you heard about it?

JKG: No.

SM: It was widely publicized in our press a year or two ago. There is a whole ministry for cotton production in Uzbekistan, which is a republic in Central Asia. This ministry was for years providing phantom cotton, nonexistent cotton, up to one or more million tons a year. This cotton was supplied to textile plants in other republics all around the country by setting up fictitious accounts and bribing the managers of those plants. Everybody involved reaped enormous illegal income in addition to their regular pay. The whole scheme wasn't serving any consumer at all; it was a pure racket, so to say.

JKG: This was shadow cotton in a shadow economy?

SM: Shadow cotton in a shadow economy. There are numerous other examples. Retail trade, including that in Moscow, the capital of the country, became, over a number of years, a particularly vicious racket with intentionally created deficits — not deficits that came out of the nature of the economy but ones that were especially created. Products unavailable to the general consumer were sold at exorbitant prices, while members of local authorities were bribed by a regular supply of really first-rate consumer goods.

JKG: Let me get this straight. The goods were sold at the higher prices, and this arrangement was greased by giving some of the supplies to the people who might know about it and otherwise take action against it?

SM: Exactly. It was greased that way.

JKG: A very plausible arrangement.

SM: A very plausible arrangement. You see, it's partly legal. If you sell consumer goods that are in deficit supply not to the general public but to people you want to sell them to — for example, the bureaucracy — at prices that are set by the state, you are doing a legal thing; there is nothing that can be charged against you. You then have the support of the bureaucracy for your illegal operations.

JKG: This is again an affirmation of our earlier point that the system provides more money to the consumer than he or she can easily spend.

SM: Yes, but let's put it this way: this is a kind of private enterprise inside the socialist system, but it's not the kind of private enterprise that promotes equality of supply and demand. It doesn't work toward increasing supply in most cases nor does it meet demand conditions through providing more goods at a higher price. If that were the case, there wouldn't be any very strong objections to it.

JKG: Let me ask you about another example that people have drawn to my attention. You have an automobile, but it's difficult to get it serviced, so a group of people get together who in their spare time service automobiles, fix tires, correct ignitions and do all the necessary things, and they get paid for it. Is that a shadow economy?

SM: No; that isn't a shadow economy. That is what is legally provided for under one of the reforms now being implemented under Mr. Gorbachev. If the group is doing it in its free time in return for additional income and not instead of its regular work, it's okay. Let me give you a better example of a shadow economy. Somebody comes to an auto repair shop, a government repair shop, to get his car repaired, but he finds a long queue there. He is told to come back in a week or a month or two months, but he is ready to pay more for having his car serviced immediately. If that's the way he gets it done, that is a shadow economy because the people who service his car are doing it not according to his position in the queue but because he is paying them extra money. The people in the repair shop are repairing his car at a higher price than is set by the government and using the government's resources for their own private enterprise without paying a cent for them. And all the while their regular wages are being paid by the government. That is a shadow economy situation.

JKG: It's still illegal?

SM: It's illegal, and it should be illegal. I don't think any private proprietor of a service station in the United States would permit a worker to use materials scot-free to provide a private service to those who are ready to pay a higher price than the one the owner had established.

JKG: That's reasonable. Now, when I was in Moscow in February of this year [1987], a senior figure in the economic establishment told me that with extensive legalization of the shadow economy, what was once corruption is now legal. He said that not everybody who was thus brought within the law and made honest is happy about it because now they have to pay taxes. Tell me about that.

SM: That's true to some extent, yes. What has happened is that a special law has been passed that permits private additional services for consumers after regular hours by workers who then pay taxes on the income received.

JKG: This is a recent law?

SM: It *is* recent; it has been in operation since May 1987, and it was adopted in November 1986. In some cases, the taxes may be too high, but the important thing, I think, is that many of the people who used to do outside extra work while they were working for the government enterprises on government time are not really ready to do that extra work in their free time. They prefer the old system, whereby they not only didn't have to pay any taxes, they had double pay.

They got wages from the government and wages from the extra work they did on the government's time.

JKG: They would prefer the shadow system without taxes to the legal system with taxes?

SM: Some of them would. It may be reasonable from their point of view.

JKG: It sounds reasonable.

4

Gorbachev: Reforms or Revolution?

JKG: We hear the changes that are currently taking place in Russia described as reforms and also as a revolution; in fact, you yourself have used the latter word. Are they reforms or a revolution, and what, I should ask, is the difference between the two?

SM: They are called reforms, but, as I've said before, you can consider them a revolution. They're not just ordinary changes in the economic organization of our society but, rather, are far-reaching and deep; they're really tantamount to sudden revolutionary change. Their principal purpose is to relieve the economy of the burden and the grasp of the bureaucracy and to do away with a shadow economy and different types of corruption and black marketeering. By doing so, they are meant to open wide the doors to personal and collective initiative, combining it with the advantages of centralized planning.

JKG: So that's what you would call revolution?

SM: It's really building up a new system instead of preserving the old one, which we have described in our last conversations.

JKG: Let us take this up in a little more systematic way. One of the things I heard you mention earlier is freedom for the enterprises. How do you define that? By enterprises, of course, we both mean the producing entities.

SM: A law has been passed recently setting up a new status for enterprises in our economy, and the main thrust of that law, which starts operating in January 1988, is to increase the freedom of decision by the enterprises.

JKG: If I go to the Soviet Union and take out Soviet citizenship, which seems somewhat improbable, I would be in a position, if I wished, to start an enterprise?

SM: No, you may want to start a small individual enterprise, but the new law to which I referred pertains to government enterprises. It provides for a change in their status that would give them more freedom.

JKG: What do you mean specifically by that freedom?

SM: Specifically, it means that the enterprise will be free to use all the income it earns, net of current costs and taxes, for capital investment, to pay bonuses to the workers as an addition to wages or salaries or for investment in the social sphere.

JKG: The latter is investment for schools, kindergarten —

SM: Kindergarten, schools and housing, clubs, cinemas.

JKG: But the decision to start an enterprise will still remain with the bureaucracy?

SM: That decision will be vested in the ministry that oversees the plan, that's true, but once the enterprise is operating, it's free to make its own decisions.

JKG: So your advice to me is not to go immediately to the Soviet Union with the idea of starting a new business?

SM: Again you are talking about a private enterprise, and that is covered by separate legislation. We are now talking about the enterprises belonging to the government. Let me proceed with those.

The depreciation that was previously distributed in a centralized manner will be retained by the plant and can be used for replacement of machinery and renovation. In fact, the enterprises, as a rule, will henceforth have to operate on an internally financed basis; they won't get centralized capital investment.

JKG: But can an enterprise set its own prices?

SM: It can in certain cases. I want to go into the price mechanism a little later.

JKG: We tend to think of freedom to set prices as fairly central to a free enterprise system.

SM: We aren't setting up a free enterprise system. We're talking about more freedom for government enterprises to make their own decisions. You have to remember that so-cialist enterprises belong to the government, and we are discussing the question of how much authority is delegated to them.

JKG: To the managers?

SM: To the managers, and to the collective direction gen-erated from within the enterprises.

Let me just say a few words on the principle of self-financing. Previously, the enterprises looked to the govern-ment for capital investment for practically all they did. Now, as a rule, capital investment will have to come from internal sources, and if those aren't sufficient, it will be necessary to apply for bank credits. Central capital investment financed through the government budget will only be retained for major capital investment projects.

JKG: Or for new initiatives?

SM: Yes, for building completely new plants or the large expansion of old ones.

JKG: So it's very important to understand that this is a liberalization within the framework of socialism and within the framework of the state's own property, the state-owned firms?

sm: The important thing is to understand that we're talking about the autonomy of government enterprises. This is somewhat comparable to the autonomy that government enterprises have in some capitalist countries. In the West some sectors have been nationalized in countries like France and Britain; this would be comparable to what happens in those sectors. Comparable but not exactly the same. It would be comparable in the sense that the income earned from the production that is sold to other enterprises or to the consumer could be used for capital investment by the enterprises, net of costs and taxes. They would make their own decisions about the distribution of their net income; that's the important thing.

jkg: One of the somber facts of our time is that the public enterprises of France, Spain and Italy — which are very numerous, as you know — tend to be a drag on those economies. They are regarded by the socialist governments in those countries as one of their misfortunes. Does that worry you?

sm: No, it doesn't. I think the drag of those enterprises is being overstated. I think many of them have become pretty profitable, and the fact that they're now being readily gobbled up by private investors during the process of privatization shows that investors deem them to be quite profitable.

jkg: I think I would differ with you on what is happening.

sm: There are, perhaps, some areas where the firms are not yet very profitable. Then they are kept within the government.

jkg: The rush to gobble up the steel and shipbuilding enterprises in Italy or Spain is not overwhelming.

sm: Those industries are in a period of long systematic stagnation even in the United States, where they are totally privately owned.

jkg: Especially in the United States, I would say. In fact,

our shipbuilding industry wouldn't exist at all if it weren't for the navy.

SM: As far as your steel is concerned, which is a big industry, it hasn't been very profitable either lately. But it belongs to the private sector, so it's not a matter of concern for the public sector.

JKG: Let's get back to the subject of the reforms. These delegate power, authority, to the individual enterprise. It will decide what and how much it will produce, how it will produce it and how it will invest for further or more efficient production. What then is left to the planning apparatus, the planning system?

SM: The range of centralized intervention into the affairs of the enterprises will be drastically reduced. Output that is intended for defense and some other centralized government needs will be obtained by the government through special contracts, and it will be obligatory for the various enterprises to honor those contracts.

JKG: Explain that a little more fully. I don't understand it.

SM: This would mean that at the beginning of every year the Gosplan — the central planning authority — and the ministries that work in coordination with it would determine what is needed by the state for defense, what is needed for centralized capital investment projects, what is needed for government consumption in other nondefense areas and so on. Contracts would then be distributed, presumably on a competitive basis, among enterprises belonging to the various branches of industry. Once the contract was signed with the enterprise, the production of the goods agreed on would be obligatory and would have priority, but it wouldn't monopolize the whole production of the enterprise; it would simply be a part of it.

JKG: Some years ago I visited the Gosplan headquarters, a rather impressive, indeed vast, organization. Will this shrink substantially in size after the reforms are fully in place?

sm: Yes. The Gosplan and many other central agencies, including the ministries, will be retained, but their staffs will be cut drastically.

jkg: We have very great difficulty in this country reducing the size of any organization. Can you cut those staffs easily?

sm: This has been done in a number of ministries already. The problem, of course, is in giving jobs in our society to those thus unemployed. They would have to be relocated to other areas, mostly in production, presumably not in administration. Many of them are qualified engineers anyhow and can work very well elsewhere.

jkg: Will they resist such relocation? Bureaucrats tend to do that, you know.

sm: I don't think so. They may, but they will have no choice.

You asked me about prices just a moment ago. The central authorities will be setting the prices of a number of major products, and those prices will be set for some period of time. They will be stable but ultimately flexible and tied to the plan. The idea is to make the enterprises interested in moving in specific directions, the ones that are determined by the overall economic strategy.

jkg: Why wouldn't it be easier just to let prices be determined by supply and demand?

sm: Because prices determined by supply and demand wouldn't reflect the strategic lines of development of the overall economic policy. Suppose we want to set up a particular kind of industry in the country or develop in a certain direction. Today's prices alone wouldn't give the information necessary to make the correct decisions. Capital investment decisions are usually made on the basis of prices that

are foreseen for some future time, so the prices set by the
central authorities would be used as a kind of indicator of
what society wants in the years to come, and that would be
a guideline for investment in the future.

JKG: You are still saying in good old socialist terms that
the public authority is wiser than the market?

SM: I am saying that the market isn't perfect in terms of
the information it provides.

JKG: I would, of course, agree with that.

SM: The corporations in a capitalist system don't base
their investment for projects that are ten or fifteen years in
the future on today's prices. They have to think about what
the future will be. That is exactly what the central authority
should do.

JKG: But there is still this basic difference between us.
You are saying that the central authority is wiser; I am reflecting some doubt as to whether that is the case.

SM: I am not saying it is necessarily wiser. I am saying
that it's not easy for the individual enterprise to foresee all
future developments, whereas a central authority is something like your large corporation: they both have the same
ability to obtain information that enables them to see and
make decisions for the years ahead.

JKG: I see your point. What you're saying is that you are
modeling socialism on General Motors.

SM: Not necessarily on General Motors, but we have a lot
to learn from corporate planning in the capitalist system.

JKG: Don't take me seriously.

Now I want to ask you, what is the stimulus at the enterprise level? What motivates the still publicly owned and publicly established enterprises?

SM: The reforms will make the workers and the managers
of the enterprises directly interested in the results of their
work, the efficiency of their plants, the upgrading of their
administration. Under the new law, incidentally, a plant

manager will be elected by the workers of the enterprise, and there will also be workers' councils that will supervise the work of the management.

JKG: Stop right there. That is something I've already heard discussed, and I have a question for you about it. I know Russian workers are very hardworking and diligent, but what happens when workers come together and elect the most agreeable, easygoing, flexible boss they can find? Isn't that a possibility?

SM: It is a possibility.

JKG: I dislike manual work, as you know. If I were a worker in a Soviet factory, I think I would want to elect the most amiable, relaxed boss possible — somebody like you.

SM: Well, I wouldn't be particularly lenient on guys like you. But the new law provides that the management that is elected by the workers in the enterprise is also subject to approval by the ministry in charge.

JKG: The system is thus still keeping a hand in there against my favorite boss?

SM: The ministry has to see that the man is qualified. But, in any case, I don't think there is really any great danger of the workers electing too easy a boss because, as I've said, the most important thing is that the workers themselves are being made more interested in the results of their work. They will be interested in the efficiency of the plant because any additional income obtained by the plant would be distributed among them as bonuses, and that would be quite an addition to their wages.

JKG: I see your point. You are gambling that the workers will vote for a manager who is in a good moneymaking mood?

SM: The manager who isn't going to be in that kind of mood is going to make the enterprise go downhill, and it will end up in bankruptcy, which is also provided for by the new law. The workers would then be unemployed. They would lose their income, and it would be a difficult situation for everybody, including both management and workers.

JKG: This gets me to another point: Does the new system allow for some unemployment?

SM: It does, but it's what you would call frictional unemployment; that is, unemployment that is the result of changing from one place of work to another. It has been suggested by a number of people in our country — and I have mentioned it before — that we should consciously increase unemployment so as to put additional pressure on the workers. This would increase their discipline in the plants and their interest in the operation.

JKG: Is this like the statement one hears in the United States that the poor must have the spur of their own poverty? You're not taking that over from us, are you?

SM: No, we aren't.

I take the view, you see, that if an enterprise operates poorly, it's not necessarily the result of poor work by the workers; it may be the result of poor management on the part of the management. Now, when an enterprise closes, the first to be hurt are the workers, who are not necessarily to blame. The unemployment thus created affects most those who are probably the least responsible for the unprofitability of the enterprise. Take the steel industry in the United States and the steelworkers. Are the steel plants being closed because the workers are unproductive, because they are lazy or unqualified, because they don't know what to do? Probably most of them are very productive, and they are working hard, but it's the general situation that puts the industry into a corner.

JKG: I agree. Our steel industry is in poor condition partly because of inferior management and partly because of the general movement of the industry to the Pacific Basin — Japan, Korea, Taiwan.

SM: Coming back to the Soviet conditions and our attempts to set up a rational system: we must realize that the workers should not be held accountable for the errors of management, whether it's the management of the enterprise or the central authority. If a planning authority puts the plant in the wrong place and then must close it, why should the workers suffer?

JKG: I think that's a reasonable point. You are saying, in effect, that you don't think of unemployment as a spur?

SM: No, we wouldn't think of unemployment as a spur. We consider the system of full employment to be an adequate system, a socially just system, an achievement of socialism, and I don't think we're going to do away with it.

JKG: Now let me come to an old Marxist point that I want to ask you about, one that is more philosophical in character. Marx talked about the alienation of labor from the means of production. No worker comes to feel responsible. Do you feel that there has been Marxist alienation in this regard in the past and that this is something that will be corrected by the reforms?

SM: When Marx wrote about alienation, he was speaking of the alienation of workers from the means of production under the capitalist system. That is because under that system capital, the means of production, belongs to another class of people. The workers are exploited by the owners, and they are not therefore interested in the result.

JKG: Do you feel that there has been such alienation in the past in the Soviet Union?

SM: Yes, in fact there has been. Marx thought that the introduction of public property in place of private property would automatically terminate that alienation. However, it so happened — and this point was recognized a few years ago when Andropov was General Secretary — that we realized that public ownership of the enterprises didn't make them automatically socialist in the full sense of the word. There is always the possibility that the workers of a particular enterprise will be alienated if their personal, material or cultural interests are not kept consistent with the interests of the enterprise. So we have a problem of making the interests of the workers coincide with the interests of the enterprise in the interest of the whole society. This is a very difficult issue, one which has to be dealt with in the future by the reforms.

JKG: That sounds pretty general to me. Can't you make it more specific? Consider me a worker and tell me how you overcome my alienation.

SM: First, you are allowed to participate in the management of the enterprise. You elect your own management. You elect the council of the enterprise, your representatives, who supervise the work of management on a day-to-day basis. In this way you come closer to participating in all the affairs of the enterprise.

Second, your wage is tied to what is called a collective contract. A collective contract is a contract that is made between the enterprise and specific groups of workers working in specific shops or on specific tasks. They work together, and they are collectively interested in what they produce. If they get good results, they get higher pay, not only their preset wages but higher bonuses as well.

JKG: Profit-sharing.

SM: Yes. But I would call it income sharing.

JKG: I understand your dislike of the word "profit-sharing."

SM: No, no. I call it income sharing in the sense that part of the income of the enterprise is distributed to the worker. Under the new law on enterprises, there are two forms, profit-sharing and income sharing. It's not a question of words; it's a question of mechanisms.

JKG: I must tell you that this distinction sounds pretty theoretical to me, but let me leave the subject with the statement that I don't fully understand the question of identification and alienation. I think a good many people in your country, as in ours, are going to go to work in the morning and come home at night without feeling much association, much sense of ownership and participation in the factory where they work. You are making workers out to be better, somewhat more amenable to social ideas, than I think they really are.

SM: The basic problem is not to make them ideal co-managers of the enterprise in the full sense but to make them more interested in the results of their own work, and I think that by providing additional stimuli, this can be done. Incidentally, there are incentives of this nature in the Japanese system, and they work.

JKG: I will leave the matter now because I don't want you to press me too hard on it when we get to the discussion of capitalism.

So, in summary, what about the role of the market? Give me a few words on what it will be under the reforms.

SM: First of all, the role of the market will be increased in the sense that every plant will have to think about finding a market for some of its products. Right now, under the old system, the enterprise isn't really responsible for marketing or selling what it produces. Once the products are made and the plan is met, it's the task of the central authority, of the bureaucracy we've been talking about, to allocate the production. The plant really doesn't have the incentive to sell its products or to find buyers. Under the reforms it will have to become more market- and consumer-oriented. It will also have to find its own supplies of materials and machinery from other enterprises instead of just applying for them from the central authority. In the new system, the central authority will not provide a plant with materials unless they are in exceedingly short supply.

JKG: Do you see a role for advertising under the new system in the selling of products?

SM: I think advertising will have to increase. We already do have some, but at this point it's really negligible. The market, not just the immediate market but the market of the future, will have to be studied. The enterprises will have to think of selling in the market from forty to fifty, maybe sixty, percent of their products — whatever remains after those government contracts I mentioned. Also the government contracts will not be for consumer goods, and so the enterprises will have to become more consumer-oriented in order to sell their nongovernment production.

JKG: You have made reference to a greater direct access to foreign markets in the Gorbachev reforms.

SM: That's true.

JKG: Explain to me what that involves.

SM: Previously any products exported from the Soviet Union had to go through the Ministry of Foreign Trade and its organizations. Now a large number of enterprises have been given direct access to the foreign market and are in a position to sell their products abroad.

JKG: So, as a practical matter, if I am a big buyer of, let us say, caviar or sealskin coats or other proletarian products of the Soviet Union, I can now go directly to the producer?

SM: Well, I don't know about caviar. Purchase of that may go through some trade organization, because most of the producers of caviar are small enterprises, but as far as large enterprises are concerned, that is so. In the foreign trade area a law has also been passed providing for the creation of joint enterprises with the participation of both our capital and capital from abroad.

JKG: We want to talk about joint enterprises later, after we've talked about capitalism and come to the means of cooperation.

SM: Also, of course, there will be more possibilities for enterprises to use their foreign income to buy goods abroad.

JKG: They won't have to turn that income in to the government, but they can use it themselves?

SM: They can use a large part of it themselves, and that will bring about more competition inside the economy. Incidentally, the point of competition is very important. One aspect of the increased role of the market in the new system will be an increase in competition between plants. Special care will be taken to avoid a monopoly position, where a single plant or a small group of plants can set higher prices for its products.

JKG: One plant will now be a norm by which the other plants will be measured. And a buyer will be able to choose between plants. Is that what you're saying?

SM: What I am saying is that if you want to buy something now, you aren't free to choose the plant from which you will get it. Under the new system you will be able to choose the plant from which you buy.

JKG: I see, yes. I think that's important.

SM: I think it's important too, but it has to be carefully promoted.

JKG: Why does it have to be carefully promoted?

SM: Because there are tendencies toward monopoly arising out of specialization within any industry. You see, our plants have been striving to mass-produce products, and in that situation you can easily come to a point where one or two large enterprises produce most of a specific product, and when this happens, you have a kind of monopoly in which there may be a price-setting mechanism.

JKG: As you have more competition between manufacturing enterprises, will that competition allow one plant to undersell another if it sees that to be an advantage?

SM: As I said, although prices of major commodities will still be set by government agencies, most prices will be the result of the market mechanism in the sense that they will be prices that are agreed upon between buyer and seller. If a plant is efficient enough to supply a good product at a lower price, of course it will be able to do so.

The market will, in fact, set the price because what, after all, is the market? The market isn't just the farmers' market where you come and buy a cucumber or something; the market is really trading between enterprises, and prices are set there in the course of direct relations between enterprises.

JKG: To go back to press the same point: Any enterprise that is more efficient and sees the opportunity for expanding its market can cut its prices under the new reforms?

SM: Yes, it can. If we're talking about products for which prices aren't set by the government agencies.

JKG: Let's catch our breath for a moment.

5

Gorbachev: Reforms or Revolution?

(Continued)

JKG: We come once again to agriculture. What are the Gorbachev agricultural reforms? What is this we hear about the role of the family farm within the collective or state farm? And what of your large food imports replacing what were once large exports?

SM: The reason we are importing more food is that per capita consumption has increased substantially in our country as compared to the consumption in Czarist Russia. The latter did, in fact, export a lot of grain to other countries.

However, if you look at how much grain we produce per capita today, it's about the same as the United States produces, just a little bit less. A lot is wasted, however, because of bad storage and other things.

Coming back to the changes in the system and the family contract you asked about: the idea is to contract out to each family part of the property of the collective or state farm so that the family can operate it and produce and use in its own interests the income from the production that it affords.

JKG: This is a step back to what we would call the owner-operated farm?

SM: I don't think that it's a step back.

JKG: A step forward, then, to the owner-operated farm?

SM: Yes. There is a conscious attempt throughout the system to reduce alienation from the means of production, in this case that of the farmers who are members of the collective farm.

JKG: I accept your correction.

SM: Incidentally, this particular reform has been put into effect in the last few years, and it has proved to be quite efficient.

JKG: So the farmer and his family have authority over what they produce and how they sell it?

SM: Yes, the farmer and his family. And also the collectives or state farms themselves. They all will be able to sell a large part of their produce — whatever they have after they have complied with the state contracts for grain — at prices not set by anybody.

JKG: When I go to Moscow, I see two classes of food stores there — those that are run by the state, by the government, where prices are relatively low, and markets where farmers, or more often their wives, are selling products from family plots at much higher prices. Will the family farm continue to sell in those markets or will they sell . . .

SM: Family farms can sell through those markets and through the cooperatives as well. Incidentally, in the markets you refer to, the farmers are selling not only the produce of their own plots but the produce of the kolkhozes, the collective farms. A large part of the kolkhoz production is sold there.

JKG: That is why they are called kolkhoz markets?

SM: Yes. And now an attempt is being made to bring more products from the collective farms to city markets, not necessarily to the kolkhoz markets but to special fairs that are being organized in the cities. There the kolkhozes can sell their produce directly to the public.

JKG: I have heard that in the past the major problems of Soviet agriculture were the failure to get farm supplies, including fertilizer, to the farms; the failure to get good operating tractors to the farms; and the inefficiency in the purchase and sale of farm products. How are these matters being corrected or have they been corrected?

SM: The idea is that most of the tractors, fertilizer and other production materials that the farms need will now be bought in the market from firms that sell them. It's going to be a market situation; that's where the market will come in.

We will discuss the role of the market later when we talk about the future of socialism. But going on from the subject of agriculture, let me tell you that there are some people who suggest that the market should also be used more in other areas, as, for example, in medical services and/or housing.

JKG: There should be a charge for medical services?

SM: Yes, and also rent should be increased in housing. Right now rents are low and subsidized. However, I would disagree with such changes. I don't think the population is ready to pay for those services, and I think the quality of medical care and of housing would be better served by putting more investment directly into them rather than by charging the consumer a higher price for them. The people pay taxes to the government, and that taxation could be used to expand the medical services.

JKG: There are certain parallels between that position and what would be popular in this country. Higher charges for Medicare aren't popular here either.

SM: The point is that if you introduce charges for medical

services and for other services which are now provided free by the public service sector and if you increase rent, you will have to increase wages, and this will become an additional burden on the enterprises. It will be a kind of vicious circle, and I don't see that it will change anything for the better.

JKG: You are saying that you're content with a mixed economy?

SM: No, I am content with a situation where medical services are free, more or less, and house rent is low, which is what most of the people want at the moment.

JKG: The disruptive results of changes in rent would be too great?

SM: The disruptive effects would be too great, and I don't think that's a useful thing.

JKG: Let me summarize: Am I right in thinking that the basic idea of the Gorbachev reforms is the encouragement of private initiative within the larger framework of a socialist economy? Is that an accurate description?

SM: Yes, I think it is. I think we want to have more private enterprises serving those areas and those spheres of consumer demand for products and services that aren't adequately served by the government enterprises; the government enterprises should feel more competition from private entrepreneurs. In this way, we will be able to increase the supply of all goods and services.

JKG: Perhaps I might put that in practical terms. Once again I become a Soviet citizen. I can't set up a plant to manufacture motorcycles or automobiles. Can I set myself up servicing automobiles or running a laundry or a restaurant?

SM: If you're a private person, you can join with other private people in a cooperative arrangement — a cooperative or a partnership — to do what you propose or you can work on your own.

JKG: Do I have to get permission?

SM: The important thing is that you can't hire labor.

JKG: Do I have to get the permission of the state to start my restaurant?

SM: You have to get the permission of the state and pay for that permission.

JKG: How long does it take me to get permission, as a practical matter?

SM: As a practical matter, I don't think it takes long, provided you are willing to pay the price.

JKG: How high is the price?

SM: It may be large; it depends on the kind of business you are in. Prices are different, and there are different forms of payment. You may pay a fixed rate once a year for permission to operate your enterprise or you may pay taxes on your income.

JKG: Doesn't that suggest that even with the reforms, there is still a reluctance to allow the individual to work on his own? He can't hire people, he has to get permission to start his business and he has to pay a substantial price for that permission. Doesn't that show a certain considerable reluctance?

SM: Private enterprises that hire people to work are capitalist enterprises, and by law they are not permitted in the Soviet Union. In one area there is an exception, and that is in joint enterprises with foreign capital. These you may consider a kind of mixed socialist-capitalist venture with a foreign capitalist or private firm in partnership with a Soviet enterprise.

JKG: Why, without interfering with the broad structure of socialism, can't you allow someone to open a restaurant and hire a few workers, open a laundry and hire a couple of assistants? The Hungarians do it; the Poles do it. What is the reason for not permitting it in the Soviet Union?

SM: We haven't had private enterprise since the 1920s, and there is quite a reluctance on the part of the Russian people to allow it again.

JKG: Doesn't this suggest that the Soviet system is a bit closed on these matters? After all, what is a restaurant keeper or a laundry man going to do to damage the larger morals of the socialist state? You aren't afraid of them as capitalists, are you?

SM: Once this kind of thing becomes widespread, a new social class of small capitalists is set up.

JKG: Very small.

SM: It will be a small class, but they will be capitalists.

JKG: I can understand why you might fear a Boone Pickens. But I don't understand why you're afraid of the man in our local Vermont store.

SM: We aren't afraid of him if he works with his family or with his partners. When he starts hiring labor, there's no telling where it will stop. Today he will hire five people, tomorrow ten, and then in a couple of years he may have one hundred people working for him. It's going to go the way capitalism went in the past. I don't see any point in going back to capitalism if the socialist system can prove it has more advantages, if it can become more efficient.

JKG: I accept your point. You are saying you still have a strong theological commitment to socialism?

SM: I have a strong commitment to socialism.

JKG: The word "theological" bothers you?

SM: We believe that one of the advantages of socialism is that if people work for other people, they feel themselves somewhat second-class citizens; there is a division between owners and workers, rich and poor. I don't see why we should try to reestablish the old division between the rich and the poor when the elimination of that division was one of the great achievements of our revolution.

JKG: I won't press you any further on that except to say

that you don't seem to object to one government servant
working for another government servant, one bureaucrat
working for another bureaucrat.

sm: The bureaucrat doesn't necessarily gain materially
from having another bureaucrat work for him. If he does
gain, it's illegal.

jkg: All right, I'll subside. There are some other questions I want to ask you about the reforms.

sm: Sure, go ahead, but let me come back to our previous
point just a moment. You can have a cooperative enterprise
with only ten people. That doesn't differ much from a private enterprise — from an entrepreneur who has hired labor.
What's the difference?

jkg: What I recognize here is that, in spite of the reforms,
I still run up against a stone wall that cannot be breached —
a stone wall that is called socialism.

sm: Socialism *is* a solidly built stone wall, and that explains
the nature of the reforms. They are meant to try to improve
it, use its advantages, not tear it down and go back to capitalism. You're right; I think you have pointed your finger
at the essence of the reforms.

jkg: Let me ask a couple of final questions. As we consider
these reforms, there is one circumstance that becomes clear.
You are allowing a lot of people to get the rewards from
service enterprises, at least as long as they don't hire other
people and thereby become exploiters of the masses. You
are greatly enlarging the whole role of self-interest. Isn't
there a problem in trying to combine the ethic of self-interest
with the ethic of socialism, the ethic that presumes that
everybody works for the common good? I ask this question
because we have had some adverse experience here in the
United States. A certain number of people every year bring
the ethic of self-interest into the local, state or federal government and see their political jobs as a way of making
money. We call this corruption. Now, as you enlarge the

area of self-interest in the Soviet Union, won't you have a similar problem?

sm: I don't think so. I think it will be less of a problem because socialism, just like capitalism, is built on self-interest. The worker doesn't work for the socialist society as a whole. He has to work for himself; he does work for himself. The basic principle of distribution in a socialist society is that goods and services are distributed according to the labor that has been rendered by the individual. So, in principle, the better he works, the higher his income and the larger his access to his reward. His personal interest, his self-interest, is to satisfy his own needs. The trick and the problem is to combine that self-interest with the interests of the state as a whole and the interests of the collective or the enterprise as a whole. How do you make them coincide or make them work together? That is the difficulty.

jkg: You recognize the difficulty is there, then?

sm: Yes, but it's at a different level than you suggest. If the worker becomes interested in the results of his production even though he doesn't own the various means of production personally — they are owned by the state — he feels that they are his to a certain extent. He is a co-owner of the enterprise, and he gets part of the profits or the income gained by that enterprise. The machinery and the materials that are used in production are also his in a sense; they aren't just nobody's materials as he might think if he were alienated from them or not really interested in what the enterprise does. If he thinks only about himself and he wants to maximize his own self-interest, then he may steal materials and other things from the plant. Or he may spend his time at the plant doing things for a private customer with the use of government materials and government equipment. This would also be self-interest, but it would be his personal self-interest, not that of the plant or the society. Perhaps our problem is the same as yours, but it's at a different level.

You, I gather, are talking more about people of private means who enter government service and are corrupt. Is that right?

JKG: Yes, perhaps. But let me be much more specific. I come to the Soviet Union to open that restaurant, and I become quite rich. How does that fit within the socialist framework? Are you going to allow me to become very rich?

SM: How are you going to become very rich if you're operating a restaurant on your own, probably with the help of your wife? I think you may be well off, but I don't think you'll get particularly rich. People don't get rich operating a restaurant as a family business.

JKG: So you don't see that as a problem?

SM: I don't think that it's a serious problem. People get rich by manipulating large sums of other people's money, basically.

JKG: Now I want to ask about the relationship between the reforms, *glasnost* and political democracy. How do these fit together?

SM: *Glasnost*, which is openness, and democracy are seen as very important means of controlling the bureaucracy and preventing it from pursuing interests that may not be those of the collective or of the country. *Glasnost* relates to the political sphere, of course. But as it appears in the newspapers of the Soviet Union and on television, it is currently being aimed to a large extent at various deficiencies in the operation of the economic system.

JKG: So this is a new system of criticism?

SM: It's a new system of public control over the operation of central and local authorities, taking them to task for things they shouldn't have done or shouldn't do. There are many instances, for example, in which local authorities in their day-to-day operations have been interfering with the operations of collective farms or even private farmers.

JKG: So they have become an object of public criticism?

sм: Yes, severe public criticism. This summer there have been a lot of articles criticizing the local authorities for not being forthcoming in promoting personal initiative in agriculture and other spheres. You have mentioned private restaurants and other private ventures. In many areas the local authorities have been quite bureaucratic in their attitude toward such enterprises; they have pursued a policy that has prohibited the free display of initiative by not providing assistance to such restaurants or repair shops and by setting taxes too high on private services, private operations and so on. They are being taken to task.

jкg: Are you saying, then, that *glasnost* has become an instrument of the economic reforms?

sм: I think it's an instrument of the economic reforms, and I think it's another example of the conscious effort to expand democracy. It's an example, like the provision for the election of plant management I mentioned earlier. The latter is a kind of compromise, I agree. The plant manager has to be elected by the workers, but at the same time he has to be approved by the ministry. It's a compromise, a kind of compromise, between the interests of central planning and the interests of the workers. It's a conscious effort to combine the interests of all those people who work in the plant with the interests of the state. One of the reasons why the economic reforms of the late 1950s and early 1960s failed was that those reforms weren't coupled with the spread of democracy. Democracy and economic reforms are necessary complements to one another.

jкg: Have we missed any other features of the Gorbachev reforms which should be stressed or have we covered them pretty well?

sм: I think they've been pretty well covered.

6

Capitalism in Review

sm: We have gone through some of the advantages and problems that have been encountered by modern socialism. Now, what about capitalism? How would you perceive the main directions of capitalist development in the last few decades?

jkg: You have dealt with enough exponents of capitalism to know that I'll say it is perfect, it has no problems and it is the inevitable future.

sm: That's what I expected when I came to discuss these questions with you, but won't you go ahead and explain what you mean?

jkg: If pressed, I will. We have a certain number of people who call themselves scholars of capitalism, who insist that it had a virgin birth in 1776 with Adam Smith, and it hasn't changed since. But I would urge that we must see capitalism, as we have seen socialism, as being in a constant process of transformation.

sm: You sound to me like a Marxist.

jkg: Joseph Schumpeter described Marx as one of the greatest scholars of all time, and I am frank to tell you I consider him too important a figure to be monopolized by you socialists and communists.

SM: Marx himself came to say that, thank God, he was not a Marxist.

JKG: At one time in his later life.

SM: That's right.

JKG: But let me say a word about the process of transformation. In the early stages of capitalism — after the Industrial Revolution in the latter part of the eighteenth century — there is no question that, as Marx said, the productivity of mankind was enormously affected. The factory system, the capitalist design, lifted industrial production to levels that had never been reached before.

SM: Lenin once noted that capitalism was a system with an unlimited urge for expansion in output.

JKG: I accept that to some extent. But by the end of the nineteenth century and the beginning of the twentieth, the system had also produced, to use a now familiar phrase, a massive alienation of the industrial workers and some other groups of people.

This was the result of the great power that it reposed in the owners or capitalists and the minimal power that the workers had. And also of the extraordinary hardships to which it subjected a few unfortunate groups. The old were discarded without income. Workers were discarded without any compensation when they weren't needed. Women, particularly, were exploited. Also children. And there were, in fact, many essential tasks — housing, health care, transportation — that capitalism didn't perform well at all.

SM: Marx summed it up once when he said that capitalism expropriated most of the population, and it was the task of the working class to expropriate the expropriators.

JKG: As you may guess, I don't entirely accept that. However, there soon followed four developments which, I venture to think you may agree, Marx did not foresee. One of them was the growth of the trade unions, which did a great deal to equalize the power between the employer and the employee. A second was the development of the welfare state, which goes back to the 1880s in Germany.

SM: Isn't it true that the trade unions were fairly early in the history of capitalism?

JKG: It depends. They came much earlier in some countries than in others. They were very late in the United States.

SM: Britain had a trade union movement as early as the middle of the last century.

JKG: Yes, but in the United States the trade union movement didn't get fully under way until the years of the Great Depression.

SM: Marx and Engels, and Lenin after them, always considered the creation of trade unions to be a new form of class struggle against the system of exploitation under capitalism.

JKG: I try to be agreeable, but I can't accept everything that you urge from Marx and Engels. That statement, for example, is nonsense.

SM: Would you perhaps say a few words about why you think it isn't true?

JKG: The trade unions didn't seek the overthrow of the system, if that's what you imply. They introduced a new support to the working class and did a great deal to equalize power as between capitalists and workers, as I've just said.

SM: Would that mean that the worker was getting full compensation for the labor power he expended in participating in production?

JKG: It's a subjective question as to what full compensation is. You are endeavoring to get me to say that there was surplus value that the worker didn't get even after the trade unions came into existence. These, again, are theoretical points I don't accept.

SM: But let's go along with the welfare state. You were

starting to say that it appeared in the 1880s. Do you refer
to Bismarck?

JKG: Yes, it started under Bismarck, and it developed in
consequence of the revolutionary sentiment of the German
working class, which was, politically speaking, perhaps the
most highly developed working-class community in the world
at the time.

SM: You may recall that Engels made fun of Bismarck's
welfare state by calling it Prussian socialism.

JKG: That I didn't know. I yield to you on knowledge of
Marx and Engels.

Then in Britain in 1910 and 1911 with Lloyd George and
in the United States with the New Deal and the Social Security Act of 1935 came another transformation in capitalism. This was an effort, largely if not completely successful,
to address the particular cruelties of the system and, eventually, its defaults in such areas as public housing, medical
care and, of course, education. No one can suppose that
capitalism would have survived without those attempts to
remedy what was wrong.

SM: Are you talking about the beginnings of the welfare
state in the United States?

JKG: I am saying that the welfare state, which also was
late in coming to the United States, had its great beginning
there in 1935.

SM: I see. Would you agree that perhaps the welfare state
is a kind of creeping socialism, a socialist form that is developing inside the capitalist system in the same way we see
certain private and capitalist forms developing inside the
socialist system?

JKG: I wouldn't worry about the terminology. To call this
creeping socialism is a common reactionary reference in the
United States. I would prefer to say that this was an absolutely indispensable design for saving capitalism. Capitalism

wouldn't have survived if it hadn't had the rough, harsh edges taken off it by the welfare state.

SM: So you don't feel that capitalism was, in this instance, masquerading in the costume of socialism?

JKG: If you are saying that capitalism took over some of the benign qualities of socialism, I will concede.

Finally, to get back to the transforming influences: the third came in the 1930s, partly with the writing and influence of John Maynard Keynes. Throughout the nineteenth century and into the twentieth, the great problem of capitalism had been the increasing severity of the business cycle, booms and busts, or what Marx called the capitalist crisis. I am making all kinds of concessions to you on Marxist terminology.

SM: I don't mean to force you to make any concessions on terminology. Perhaps you could say a few words on why the depressions became deeper. My own view is that a lot of that had to do with the multiplication of the big corporations, the ground for which wasn't really prepared in terms of mass demand. Mass demand couldn't match the mass production that came with the large corporations, so this brought a lot of instability to the system and perhaps was one of the causes of the Great Depression of the 1930s.

JKG: I broadly agree with that. As the system developed, income wasn't paid out in sufficient quantities. There wasn't enough widely distributed income to buy the products. That's an oversimplification, but it's the essence of the matter.

There was, indeed, a great capacity to produce; there was much less capacity to provide and secure the flow of income that could buy what was produced.

SM: Would you also say that the large corporations, or big business in general for that matter, brought about quite a lot of difficulties for the numerous small businesses, including the farmers? (Here I am using Western terminology;

in Marxist terminology we would call the large corporations monopolies.)

JKG: Let me say a word about that in just a minute, may I?

SM: Sure.

JKG: It's a very important point.

SM: I think so.

JKG: This third development in the transformation of capitalism came, as I've said, with Keynes. It was the assumption by the state of responsibility for the level of production in the economy, and it happened in all the industrial countries. The basic design was that the government budget would compensate for any shortcomings — any deficiencies — in private spending. When there was a shortage of aggregate demand in the economy in relation to what could be produced, the state would step in. By lowering taxes or increasing expenditures or a combination of the two, it would increase demand, increase production and bring the economy back to full employment. That was the basic idea of the Keynesian revolution.

SM: Wasn't there much more to it, for example the reform of the Stock Exchange? I recall that the first commissioner of the Securities and Exchange Commission was President Kennedy's father, who was himself a famous, if not infamous, stock exchange manipulator in the 1920s. Thus Roosevelt, following Keynes's ideas or maybe coinciding with them, brought in the rich or part of the rich capitalist class to reform capitalism.

JKG: That's an interesting but not terribly important point in my judgment. There is no doubt, however, that Roosevelt, in appointing Joseph P. Kennedy to police Wall Street, had the idea that the fox would discipline not only the chickens but the other foxes.

SM: But Joseph Kennedy was considered at the time a traitor to his class, wasn't he?

JKG: And there were quite a few others. Averell Harriman, for example, and Roosevelt himself. But let's not exaggerate that point. It appeals to your journalistic sense rather than to your economic side.

SM: No, what I'm saying is important. It is that the capitalist class found itself at that point capable of producing people who saw further than their own interest in the immediate profit or the immediate speculation. This helped bring about reforms in capitalism, which produced a new kind of organization.

JKG: That, I admit, is a very good and interesting point, and I agree with it.

SM: But it came from within the class, not from outside it, although it was influenced by what you have elsewhere called revolutionary sentiment.

JKG: That's quite true, but I would add as a footnote that these men had a certain combined public and personal commitment. They knew there was a public problem. Solving it they thought far more important and far more interesting than the private task of making money, of which they already had a great deal. So people like the senior Kennedy, Harriman and others who came to Washington at the time found in public service an emotional release, a sense of gratification, that they couldn't find in ordinary capitalist endeavor.

I must, however, get back to my main argument. There was a fourth development affecting capitalism in those years that I also regard as very important. It was the virtual disappearance of the old-fashioned capitalist and his replacement by the manager, the corporate bureaucrat. Two major American scholars, Adolf Berle and Gardiner Means, again in the 1930s — that intellectually very productive decade — showed that in numerous large corporations the power had passed or was passing to management. This point was taken up in the early forties by James Burnham, a most conservative economic writer, in his book *The Managerial Revolution*.

So, in some measure, the capitalist disappeared from authority, at least in his old form. Do you agree with that?

s m : I don't completely agree with it.

j k g : I thought it would involve difficulties for you.

s m : No, no difficulties. In my book *Millionaires and Managers,* which is on this subject, I argue and prove, in actual fact, that not only in the thirties but later on well into the sixties and even up to today, you have a kind of coexistence of the rich and the top managerial elite in controlling these corporations. Some corporations are controlled by the managers; some are controlled by very rich people, large stockholders; some are controlled jointly. So my main argument in that book, and I'm still convinced it's true, is that the kind of manager that succeeded as a result of your managerial revolution was really part of a capitalist class that was tied to the interests of the capitalist corporation. I think that some of your American writers were in agreement with that.

j k g : I think some may have been in agreement, but I appreciate the need of a Marxist to keep the idea of the capitalist alive.

s m : I believe the point you're making is extremely important because it touches the substance of what the continual transformation of capitalism and also socialism is all about. Capitalism is based on private property, but the private property system doesn't remain unchanged. It changes in stages. You have the individual entrepreneur as the main figure in the early stage of capitalism. Then, instead of the individual entrepreneur, comes the corporation, together with the managerial class, and then a combination of state property, state intervention and the large corporation — a kind of fusion between them. This is what a Marxist would call a state-monopoly capitalism. I'm not insisting on the terminology.

What I want to say is that these developments show great

changes and great vitality within the system, and we see similar changes under socialism. What brings them about in my view are changes in the technology of production and in the social structure of the whole system. The system then has to adjust to the changes. In the modern technological age the private entrepreneur is no longer the leading figure, and he hasn't been the leading figure since the beginning of the century.

JKG: Let me say a further word now about these developments. I believe the four transforming factors I've mentioned did a great deal to secure the future of capitalism. If plenary power over wages and working conditions had remained with the capitalists, if there had been no welfare state, if depressions had continued and got worse, if managers hadn't replaced capitalists, capitalism would not have survived. Alienation, as I said a moment ago, was already very great in the early part of this century. Now there is, broadly speaking, an acceptance of the system.

SM: Not by the trade unions, not by the working class, would you say?

JKG: Yes, American trade unions are, on the whole, very conservative.

SM: Is that right?

JKG: In many ways the American trade union movement is more conservative than I am.

SM: Meaning that they accept capitalism as a system?

JKG: They are at least as inclined to accept the capitalist system in its present form as I am.

SM: Is that because their wages are higher than, for example, the wages of workers in the developing countries?

JKG: I have no doubt that good wages lead people to a certain satisfaction with their living and working conditions. I find that good pay is even favorable to my own frame of mind.

sm: I believe I want to come back to the point about the difference between wages in the capitalist countries and those in the rest of the world, but please go on.

jkg: I repeat that, as the result of these four developments, the system came substantially to be accepted in the decades immediately after the Second World War. The war had brought the American economy back to full employment; that was the Keynesian effect of the very large public expenditures that were then necessary. There had been no great wartime inflation, something for which I'm prepared to take a measure of credit since I was the one directly in charge of price control. And the twenty-five years after World War II were a really remarkable period in the history of capitalism. Stable prices and a steady increase in production. There were only two years in those twenty-five when output didn't increase, and there was nearly full employment the whole time. This demonstrated, I would say, the broad credibility of the system.

sm: There are a few points on which I would disagree. There was, in fact, quite a lot of inflation in some European capitalist countries in that period. Not so much in the United States, although there was some inflation here during the Korean and later the Vietnam wars.

jkg: Very little by later standards.

sm: Measured by later standards, perhaps. Five or six percent at the most. But there was quite a lot of unemployment in the United States by the end of the fifties and the beginning of the sixties.

jkg: Not very much, generally around five or five and a half percent.

sm: I think it was larger than that. It came to about seven percent at the most, but it was considered then to be one of the nation's problems, and it was called by the Democratic party, I think, its number one problem at one point.

jkg: Democrats can exaggerate; even Republicans do.

SM: I agree generally that this was a period of good growth in both the United States and Europe, more so in Japan, but would you agree that a lot of this was the result of Europe and Japan striving to catch up with the United States? They had, of course, been devastated by the war, whereas the United States had rather benefited from it economically, so the Europeans and the Japanese had a lot to catch up with. And in doing so, they provided stimulus and also markets for the American economy.

JKG: I would agree that that had a role. During this period the Japanese and the Germans patronized and subsidized our capital goods industries, including our machine-tool industries. There is no question that this was important. More important, I would say, was the continuation of the generally constrictive tendencies that had caused the Great Depression. These limited inflation, and in reponse to them, the government came strongly to the support of the economy by lowering taxes, increasing social expenditure and thus maintaining demand, all very popular things.

SM: I agree with you that there were only short periods of recession in those years. However, there were also many new industries brought to life by new developments in technology and innovation. I believe they would have appeared with or without the support of the government. They would have developed at a fast rate if there had been no Keynesian revolution and no government support because they were new technologies that were competing and competing very effectively with the old ones. Would aviation not have spread without the Keynesian revolution?

JKG: Or television?

SM: Or the chemical industry or electronics?

JKG: I agree, but I would still put great emphasis on the successful role of the state in those years in maintaining nearly full employment.

SM: Wouldn't you agree that the trade unions, which managed to secure a fairly stable share of national income for their members, the working class, produced additional demand?

JKG: Absolutely.

SM: Which supported the economy in addition to what the government did?

JKG: Certainly. I think the trade union movement had a positive effect in sustaining demand.

SM: So the class struggle had a benign effect on the capitalist system at that point?

JKG: Yes, if you want to put it in Marxist terms.

SM: I was surprised in your account of the development of capitalism that you failed to mention the large part of the capitalist system that used to be the colonial system. The colonies have now become the developing countries, and many of them have largely accepted the capitalist system and are developing along capitalist lines.

I have the feeling that in the past the most developed industrial countries really benefited at the expense of the other part of the world, what is called the Third World. They had ready access to cheap labor, to cheap materials and, in general, to practically all the vast resources of the earth. These made it possible for them to develop a much higher standard of living and pay much higher wages to their workers, all of which helped the trade unions accept the capitalist system and supported its social and economic stability. Would you agree with that assessment?

JKG: Only to a limited extent. One must bear in mind that in the case of the United States, we were largely an internally supported economy until very recent times. Our foreign trade, purchases and sales alike, was very small in relation to our total gross national product. For that reason, until, say, fifteen years ago any effect of the kind of developments you cite was limited.

sm: Let me give you one example. At a certain time, tin and natural rubber were quite important for the development of American industry. I wouldn't say they were crucial, but they were important. They came from the British colonies and some of the Latin American countries such as Bolivia, and they were really relatively low priced because of the low labor costs that had been produced by the colonial conditions. If tin and rubber hadn't been available abroad at those low prices, you Americans would have had to develop your own tin and rubber industries or a substitute for those products.

jkg: I wouldn't put as much emphasis on that as you do. I do agree that in the years after World War II, the demand for our machinery and the general situation in the overseas supply of raw materials were, on the whole, beneficial to the American economy.

sm: You are talking about the American economy, but perhaps this was even more true for the European and Japanese economies.

jkg: Quite possibly.

sm: Going back to an earlier time, didn't that kind of thing lead to a scramble for colonies and at some point even to a world war — World War I? That was fought, to some extent, to acquire colonies.

jkg: You are, indeed, going back to an earlier time.

sm: Yes, because I think that was one of the reasons for the difference between the high development in Europe and the United States and the fairly low development in the other parts of the capitalist system.

jkg: I was talking about a more recent period. You're going back to Lenin's argument that the workers of the developed countries lived on the backs of the oppressed people of the colonies.

sm: Lenin had in mind the labor aristocracy, not all the

workers. Some of the workers in the advanced countries were corrupted by the monopolies, which used part of their colonial superprofits to give them higher wages.

JKG: I don't react with the same certainty to the earlier period. I don't think the United States benefited appreciably from its colonial possessions in the Philippines or Puerto Rico or even in Panama except for the canal. What you say may have had some relevance in Britain and elsewhere in Europe.

7

What Went Wrong with Modern Capitalism

sm: You've been saying a lot that is positive about the Keynesian development and the Keynesian revolution, the welfare state and the trade unions, but they aren't fashionable anymore in the capitalist world, at least not the welfare state and the Keynesian revolution. My question is, what went wrong with capitalism?

jkg: Good question. We had twenty-five good years from 1945 to 1970, and the good fortune didn't continue. There is one explanation I would like to see achieve wide currency. It is that the generation of economists responsible for all that good fortune, the generation of which I was a member, gradually got older, and a younger and less able generation came along to take over. I don't think that that analysis will be widely accepted.

sm: Although it may have something to do with what happened. Perhaps if more able Keynesians were really managing the economy now, capitalism would be more successful.

jkg: I'll be serious. Several things have now damaged the capitalist performance, some of them the same things that we mentioned earlier as damaging the socialist performance. The great corporations and the managerial revolution have bureaucratized a large part of capitalist production, and this has led to some of the same hardening of the arteries that you have identified in the socialist world.

SM: Could you give an example of the negative effects of this corporate bureaucratization?

JKG: The decline of the steel industry, of the great steel firms, in both the United States and other countries.

SM: Perhaps, in defense of your corporate bureaucracy, I should note that the situation in the steel industry is widespread throughout the world. It may be the result of new materials competing with steel or of a less material-intensive economy rather than of the failures of the corporate bureaucracy.

JKG: I wouldn't be limited to one cause, either, but if you knew well the management of heavy industry in the United States, you wouldn't doubt that there has been this corporate arteriosclerosis. When I was directing price control in World War II, I formulated what I hoped would be called Galbraith's First Law of Executive Talent. It was that all great executives come to resemble intellectually the products they manufacture. Until you had done business at length with top officers of the steel corporations, you didn't really appreciate the intellectual qualities of a billet of steel.

SM: Was this decline the result of lessening competition, of the monopoly of large corporations, or was it a product of internal ossification?

JKG: I would think the latter; however, again, one shouldn't be confined to a single explanation. There are other causes of the problems we have been encountering in the last fifteen years. Should I go on to them?

SM: Yes, but just a moment. There was a kind of superiority that the United States enjoyed in world markets in the postwar years when it didn't really have much compe-

tition from other countries. Didn't that add to the bureaucratization and stagnation of the large corporations that you've
been talking about?

JKG: Unquestionably. David Halberstam has written in
great detail about this in the American automobile industry,
showing how a kind of euphoric self-satisfaction led to its
decline.

SM: Lenin once said that lack of competition breeds stagnation; I would say the same is true of the conditions that
led to the ossification of bureaucracies. But please go ahead
to the other points.

JKG: The second adverse thing that happened to the United
States was, of course, the rising power of the new countries,
not only Japan but also Korea, Taiwan, Hong Kong, Singapore. Their industries have invaded our markets and those
of the other older capitalist countries and have had a particularly adverse effect on the old mass-production industries.

SM: Isn't it true that capitalism in the United States, Japan
and perhaps in Europe helped to create the competitive
industries in the newly industrialized countries by transferring some of the production of their large corporations to
those countries?

JKG: To some extent, but it's a point that could easily be
exaggerated. The Japanese firms, the most successful of the
new industrial firms, had very little connection with the
American multinationals.

SM: I was talking about Korea and Taiwan. I thought you
meant the newly industrialized countries. When you said
new, didn't you mean them?

JKG: I was thinking of Japan — I thought I mentioned
it. And Korea, Taiwan and Singapore haven't been all that
important as an area for transnational manufacturing corporations.

SM: I was led to believe that a lot of the industries in the newly industrialized countries were set up either by contract with transnational corporations or by licenses produced by the transnationals.

JKG: This is your Marxist conviction that corporations are all-powerful and everywhere.

SM: No, I have read a number of non-Marxist books on the subject.

JKG: Let's go on to the other causes of capitalism's worsening performance. In the last fifteen or twenty years we have also discovered internal contradictions in the Keynesian system. When the need was for the government to support the economy, the solution was very easy — lower taxes, higher spending. These were politically very popular remedies. However, in the 1970s, as you know, inflation became the problem. That evidently required lower government expenditures, higher taxes and also higher interest rates, all of which were politically unpopular. I come here to what I would describe as the political asymmetry of the Keynesian system.

SM: Isn't it true that inflation was a product of the Keynesian system itself?

JKG: No, I don't think so. But it was partly a product of one of the other four things I mentioned as favorable forces in our earlier conversation. That is the development of the trade unions.

SM: How do they affect the picture?

JKG: The trade unions had the power to raise the wages of their workers. This brought compensating price increases. The price increases then brought higher wages, and there developed in the corporate economy an independent wage-price spiral. Inflation so caused could only be checked by counterinflationary measures of great severity; it could only be checked by a lot of unemployment. That was a new factor in the situation.

SM: But weren't higher wages the result of less unemployment and less unemployment the result of the Keynesian system?

JKG: Only to a marginal extent. The higher wages reflected much more the growing strength of the trade unions in the period after World War II.

SM: But isn't it true that less unemployment helped them to achieve this goal?

JKG: I would say that the major factor in producing inflation was the interacting power of large corporations and strong trade unions. An independent wage-price dynamic. This, to repeat, could only be stopped by a lot of unemployment.

SM: Why couldn't the corporations compensate for higher wages by increasing productivity, by modernizing plant and equipment?

JKG: There you get back to one of the things we mentioned earlier, the bureaucratic ossification of the system. And, of course, the natural limits on innovation. At any given time only so many inventions are available.

SM: But this was a period of very rapid technological progress. I thought the productivity of American industry was rising at a rapid rate until the late sixties. Isn't that true?

JKG: Yes, it is. And there was some tapering off of productivity gains from roughly 1970 on. There were other reasons for this that I haven't mentioned. We were devoting too much of our technological talent and our capital to military uses.

SM: That's a very important point you are making now.

JKG: It's something I would like to ask you about at a later stage as regards the Soviet Union.

SM: Yes, let's talk about the military later, but let's come back for a moment to this point on wages. You were talking about the rigidity in wages that Keynes didn't foresee.

JKG: Not rigidity but the upward pressure on wages caused by the upward movement of prices and vice versa.

SM: Isn't it true that most of this upward pressure initially came from rising prices, not from increased wages? Wouldn't you agree, as an administrator of prices during the Second World War and an observer of prices later on, that there were a lot of what used to be called administered prices? These led to price rigidity and an upward pressure on prices as well as on wages. It wasn't just the higher wage situation, was it?

JKG: Let me be perfectly clear as to how this worked, as I see it. The modern corporation had the power to raise prices — to administer prices, if you will — rather than to have them set impersonally in the market. The unions could then raise wages to keep abreast of the price increases. The result, as I said before, was a wage-price dynamic in which wages shoved up prices and prices pulled up wages. I certainly don't want to put the full blame on the trade unions. Or, for that matter, on the corporations. I would put it on the institutional relationship between the two. May I add a word on that?

SM: Yes, please.

JKG: It's very interesting to note that some countries were successful in controlling this tendency.

SM: You mean the wage-price spiral?

JKG: The wage-price spiral. I suppose the best case is Austria and its Social Market Policy. The Austrians make it a matter of formal public policy to limit wage claims to what can be afforded from the existing price structure and to see that the corporations don't take advantage of this restraint. But there are also less formal approaches in other countries — Japan, Germany and Scandinavia. By keeping their hands off the wage-price dynamic, the English-speaking countries are, to some extent, the exceptions. And they are suffering for it.

SM: I see. I am impressed by your analysis of the asymmetry in the Keynesian approach. Keynesianism is really meant, it seems, for a period when there is mass unemployment and low inflationary pressure. It turns out that the Keynesian system isn't so valid with the existence of large corporations and large trade unions.

JKG: Union and corporate power make it less viable for dealing with inflation.

SM: You mean it isn't easy and agreeable to regulate or control the new system by Keynesian methods? You have to have something more than the simple tools that were suggested by John Maynard Keynes?

JKG: Absolutely.

SM: But isn't it true, though, that it would be premature to throw the baby out with the bath water and throw Keynesian economics out of the arsenal of weapons used by the state? Look at monetarism and neoconservatism in economic policy. Aren't they even more simplified prescriptions for regulating the economy?

JKG: I find myself in full agreement on that. The political difficulties with Keynesian policy — the difficulty in raising taxes and cutting expenditures, the added difficulty from the wage-price spiral — led both the United States and Britain to search in the late seventies and early eighties for a magic, painless formula to solve our problems with inflation. The magic we found was monetarism. Leave everything to the central bank. Fix the supply of money, adjust it only as the economy increases, and the problem is solved. You won't be surprised to discover that I'm not a monetarist.

We learned in the early eighties that this magic, to the extent that it works at all, works only as it produces a very large amount of unemployment and much idle plant capacity. And another important point, one we haven't yet recognized fully: it works only as it very severely weakens the employing corporations.

SM: Would you explain that in more detail?

JKG: Yes. Monetarism, working through very high interest rates, cuts back on the investment of the corporations. The high interest rates also encourage an inflow of foreign funds that bid up the dollar, make imports cheap and further weaken our steel, automobile and other industries. It follows that the trade unions can then no longer claim wage increases without risking a shutdown of the employing corporations. So, instead of winning wage increases, they have to negotiate give-backs. This, as in the case of the steel industry, is necessary just to keep the corporations alive. That's the way monetarism works. It does stop inflation, but we have discovered that it's a remedy that is considerably worse than the disease it seeks to cure.

sm: Wouldn't you agree that, along with all the deficiencies of monetarism, there were other causes for the slow-down in the capitalist system in the seventies and eighties? There were the increase in fuel prices and the change in the structure of the economies, with the movement away from the basic industries. This meant stagnation in a lot of industries that had once been leaders while others, like the microchip and microcomputer industries, biotechnology and the development of new materials, were in a new boom. Didn't all these factors together help bring about a period of very slow growth that is still continuing?

jkg: I would agree with that, yes. There was, however, some exaggeration of the effect of the increased oil prices on both inflation and industrial performance. Those in charge of economic policy didn't do very well under the Carter administration, and there is a well-recognized tendency among economists to look for scapegoats. So it was convenient to blame our problems on the Arabs and OPEC. But I would agree that the shifting structure of the economy *was* a factor. This was occurring not exclusively in the technological area, as you suggest, but also in a very large range of other activities.

sm: For example?

JKG: There was a shift toward entertainment, television, services in general. After things work well, people want them to look well, so the arts became important. That's something that isn't fully recognized yet.

SM: What I want to underscore here, in complete agreement with you, is that monetarism is an oversimplified theory not only as it affects overall macroeconomic management but as it absolutely ignores deep structural changes, including those you have mentioned.

JKG: I'm glad to hear that. I take it monetarism isn't going to become a fad in the socialist world.

SM: I don't think it will. But let me press you a little further on this. Don't you give the monetarists too much blame for the disastrous results of certain policies that have recently been pursued? Isn't it true that there were other schools of thought that came to light as a result of the demise of Keynes?

JKG: I'm not prepared to speak of the demise of Keynes. I *am* prepared to speak of the difficulties that Keynesian policy has encountered. And I want to give the monetarists full credit for their contribution to our present problems.

SM: But what about supply-side economics and what is called Reaganomics, which really combines monetarism, supply-side economics, budget balancing and so on?

JKG: I was afraid you would mention supply-side economics. I think this gives you a certain advantage in dealing with capitalism.

SM: In what way?

JKG: Supply-side economics was never meant to be taken seriously. It was the work of an economist from California by the name of Arthur Laffer.

SM: Does that come from the word "laugh"?

JKG: No, though there might be a connection. Professor Laffer showed that if no taxes are collected, the government gets no income, which is true. He also showed that if taxes are at a one hundred percent rate — if the government takes all the income — nobody would pay them, and that is true. He then drew a freehand curve between the two extremes and said that there was a certain point, which he selected arbitrarily, at which, if taxes were reduced, more revenue would be raised. His analysis wasn't something that economists took seriously.

SM: But I do accept Laffer's concept to a certain extent. I would say that in the case of the current reforms in the Soviet Union, the lowering of taxes on the income of the enterprises certainly would create a greater supply of products due to more initiative on their part and on the part of their workers.

JKG: There is no indication in the United States that high taxes, either on personal incomes or on corporations, were, in fact, a bar to increased production.

SM: Why were the taxes reduced then?

JKG: The taxes were reduced for the benefit of the affluent, but as former Budget Director David Stockman indicated, it's never possible to admit to this in a democracy such as ours; you have to have a cover story. And, as Mr. Stockman pointed out, supply-side economics was the cover story for reducing taxes on the affluent. I hate to make this concession, but we're struggling here for the truth, and that is the truth.

SM: Is it also true that taxes were reduced for corporations? I'm talking now about Reaganomics.

JKG: That's a good correction. Overall, looking at the whole period, taxes were substantially reduced on private incomes, but they weren't reduced effectively on corporations. They are somewhat lower but not much.

SM: Isn't it true that the tax on corporations is now about thirty-four percent or is going to be thirty-four percent instead of forty-six?

JKG: It's difficult to answer that because there was a closing of a wide number of corporate loopholes so that it isn't certain that the corporate tax has come down very much. Indeed, some argue that it has been increased.

SM: When I was writing *Millionaires and Managers,* the effective rate of taxation actually paid by the richest families in the United States, those with an income of over one million dollars a year, was one half the official tax rate. If the official top tax rate was in the area of seventy percent, they paid about thirty-five percent due to loopholes.

JKG: I think that's entirely possible, but there were always some that paid the full marginal rates.

SM: But surely the supply-side theory isn't a new theory at all. Wasn't it the Keynesians who were always saying that by lowering taxes, we could provide more stimulus to the economy?

JKG: That position was taken by some Keynesians; I wasn't one of them. Indeed, in the early sixties, I was involved in a sharp dispute with a great friend of mine, the late Walter Heller. He was for reducing taxes, and I was for stimulating the economy by having higher — and much-needed — social expenditure.

SM: I think in that discussion you were perhaps more correct than your opponent. If one looks at the results of Reaganomics, I think one would agree that lower taxes have only led to higher deficits, not to higher output.

JKG: I think that's true.

SM: Wouldn't you agree with me that the result of Reaganomics has been devastating deficits in the federal budget and also in the balance of payments? And, at first, quite a large amount of unemployment? The unemployment rate has been going down recently in the United States, but it's still as high as ten percent in Western Europe, where similar neoconservative policies have been pursued.

JKG: I'm not a supporter of Reagan economics, and I will, in due course, suggest what I trust will be thought some very wise alternatives.

SM: There is another effect of neoconservatism that I would like to mention, and that is that the lower growth rate and the budget deficit have helped to create a movement against the welfare state. I'm now referring to what is popularly known as the crisis of the welfare state, the attempt to reduce social payments wherever possible while at the same time military expenditures are growing. Do you feel that this is also one of the salient features of the current difficulties caused by monetarism and conservative economics?

JKG: It's a point I have frequently made; I might, indeed, accuse you of reading some of my past writing. I have attacked the notion that here in the United States the rich have not been working because they have had too little money and the poor have not been working because they have had too much. The welfare state has also suffered from its own success. As people are assured of income in their old age, of unemployment compensation, of other welfare services, and as family incomes get higher, there is a certain tendency for people to become more conservative. This weakens the political commitment, the compassion, the fear, that gave us the early welfare state.

SM: Under socialism we have people who suggest that our own welfare state be reduced by reducing free medical services, free education, low-cost housing and other public services. Such people call themselves progressive reformists. In your case they are called conservatives and reactionaries.

JKG: I'm prepared to accept that difference in terminology.

SM: Isn't it worth noting that they are called such different names on the two sides of the line that separates the systems? But now let me again raise the subject of concentration. You know that Marx wrote about concentration, and we have seen it getting to the point that large corporations have taken over a major part of the business in capitalist countries. How do you see concentration at present?

JKG: I take it as inevitable in our economy. In the case of the United States somewhere around two thirds of all production comes from one thousand to two thousand large corporations. And this is generally the situation in all the industrial countries. Marx thought that eventually there would be so few corporations, they would be easily overturned — it would be the end of the system — but I don't think that prediction is being borne out as regards capitalism.

SM: I recall that Lenin, when he pursued that particular subject, indicated that monopolies or large corporations are unable to eliminate small or medium-sized businesses. So the two coexist, and this creates a certain conflict and contradiction between the two parts of the economy, one tending to have monopoly-administered prices and the other representing the old world of free competition.

JKG: You mean there is a coexistence between the entrepreneurial businesses and the great managerial corporations?

SM: Exactly.

JKG: I accept that, but I regard it as inevitable and something we can live with.

SM: Meaning that you don't feel that the large corporations operate at the expense of small business?

JKG: Not particularly. I have a lot of problems to worry about, and I'm very happy to put that one wholly aside.

SM: But the problem does exist?

JKG: I'm not at all sure that it does.

SM: Now, one form of concentration I have been looking at in recent years is the emergence of transnational corporations and also of transnational banks. I think modern capitalism has now moved toward a situation where a large part of the total business of the capitalist world is being done by these large global enterprises, whose interests are transnational rather than national. I feel that this creates a danger to the nation-state and to its economic policies. Do you agree with that proposition?

JKG: Many of my liberal friends, liberal in the American sense, spend a lot of time worrying about the transnational corporations, sometimes called the multinationals. I don't. I believe them to be an inevitable feature of capitalism. I rather applaud their tendency to create what amounts to an international civil service and to reduce some of the more obtrusive features of national sovereignty. Throughout the last century and in the first half of this one, we suffered enormously from the conflict between sovereign states, and the big industries on each side profited greatly thereby. Today, when IBM is doing business in both France and Germany, it isn't going to relish conflict between those two countries the way the big steel companies did a hundred years ago.

I yearn for the day when we have multinational corporations operating as between the Soviet Union and the United States.

SM: There are two sides, I think, to the transnational issue. One is the internationalization of economic life, which is a trend to which we cannot object. It's a tendency of the future, and that wave cannot be turned back.

However, there are many negative features in the way the transnational corporations operate. One, for example, is their tendency to overlook the social problems that exist in this or that country. There have been many times in the last few years when transnational corporations have closed plants in a particular country without any regard for the prevailing employment situation and transferred production to another country, sometimes one with lower-cost labor, sometimes just because the overall business situation in the first country wasn't favorable.

Now, I think you would agree that such an action does

seriously affect the employment policies of the countries in question; it creates a lot of difficulties. I realize that some of those difficulties may arise out of real business problems, but they should be discussed with the national governments and the relevant trade unions; the interests of the various parties involved shouldn't be ignored.

JKG: I agree that there should be consultation with the unions and with the government. This is particularly important here in the United States because in these last years we have suffered a great deal from the movement of plants out of our country and into countries with lower production costs, including those of the Pacific Basin and, most recently, Mexico. However, as I said earlier, the greatest concern in these instances should be that the workers who lose their jobs be made secure in their income. If they are of mature years, that income should be for life. Others, who are younger, should be helped by retraining or with relocation. I am prepared, however, to accept this plant movement between countries as one of the inevitable features of the system.

SM: Isn't it true that when a national government pursues a policy of full employment or relatively full employment, or even just a Keynesian policy of supporting or adding to aggregate demand so as to mitigate the effects of cyclical recessions, the actions of transnational business, which may be in total disregard of those policies, create additional problems by making the national governmental regulations less effective?

JKG: I don't think so.

SM: What would be your argument in that case?

JKG: I don't believe that the response of the great corporation, including the international corporation, to an increase in aggregate demand or to a diminution of aggregate demand with the resulting effect on employment is different from the response of the small entrepreneurial enterprise.

SM: I must take exception to that. The small enterprise

is in its national territory and will remain there. It has no other way to act than to try to continue its operation within the nation's boundaries, whereas the transnational corporation would be willing to close its plants in case of recession and completely forgo output in the particular country, making it much more difficult for the government of that country to support aggregate demand and full employment.

JKG: Like many of my liberal friends, you have the transnational corporations too strongly on your mind. We will have to agree to disagree.

SM: This is obviously a point of disagreement, but I would like to say that it's also a point of great concern for a number of countries, especially for the smaller ones. Living as you do in the United States, which accounts for a large part of the output of the capitalist world, you perhaps don't feel the effects of transnational corporations as deeply as people in other countries do. And they *are* concerned. Their concern is, in fact, reflected in the creation of a number of bodies within the United Nations, such as the Committee and Centre on Transnational Corporations. Nations in Europe and all over the world are trying to set up a code of conduct for the transnationals.

Your opinion is different, and I respect it, but I just want to state that there is a difference here.

Let me add one final point. You say that the transnational corporations create a kind of international civil service. That remark to me is fairly strange in view of the way you denounced the corporate bureaucracy in one of our previous discussions. Isn't your international civil service the same kind of bureaucracy but on an international scale? It can be very restrictive and very static, leading to stagnation in the world economy, not just in the economy of a single capitalist country like the United States.

JKG: I grant part of your point. When I want to speak well of an international body, I call it an international civil service, but if I wanted to speak badly about it, I would, of course, call it an international bureaucracy.

However, my larger point still stands: this is an organization that crosses the barriers of national sovereignty, and that is something I generally favor. To repeat what I said earlier: the world has suffered excessively in the past from the defense of national sovereignty.

sm: You're not worried by the fact that Japanese banks are buying up some banks on Wall Street or that Japanese firms are buying up some firms in the United States? Shouldn't a British citizen be worried that half of the City of London has been bought by international investors, making the banks there less interested in the future of the British economy, more interested in the world as a whole — all to the detriment of British industry?

jkg: Not especially. I would be more concerned to correct some of the present practices of our own banks and thrift organizations, as we call them. And later I'll mention a more fundamental remedy. That is to correct our trade balance so that we don't put so much money into the hands of the Japanese, much of which they then invest back in this country.

sm: My other concern is that transnational corporations, especially American transnational corporations, tend to support the superpowerism of the United States. The fact that the United States has created a global economic empire and by means of transnational corporations is spreading its activities around the world seems to support the overall contention by the United States government that it is a superpower because of its global interests.

jkg: I'm afraid on that point I have to charge you with being gravely obsolete. And you, in effect, have admitted it yourself. A few minutes ago you were frightening me about the Japanese banks and the Japanese multinationals. Now you're telling me that we should be concerned about the power of our own banks and multinationals. I still think you're too fixed on this subject.

SM: I see that you're not worried about the problem of the transnational corporation, and I understand your attitude, but I don't see that you give any reasonable arguments in favor of your position. Perhaps we should go on and discuss other issues since we seem not to be finding an understanding on this one.

JKG: That's a useful suggestion.

8

"The Galbraith Reforms"

SM: In an earlier conversation we talked extensively about the economic reforms or the Gorbachev revolution in the Soviet Union. May we turn now to the possibility for change in the United States? I don't see any kind of revolution in this country except the Reagan revolution or what is claimed to be the Reagan revolution. Would you call it that, and would you perhaps suggest a different set of proposals? "The Galbraith reforms," perhaps?

JKG: I have been reluctant to attribute the word revolution to the changes that have occurred with Mr. Reagan. I think they are temporary in the history of capitalism; supply-side economics and monetarism are transitory steps and will disappear from sight. I would much prefer in our present discussion to center on the things that should be done to secure the future of the system. I rejoice in the reference to the Galbraith reforms, but I must point out to our readers that it is your terminology, not mine. I want to ensure my reputation for extreme modesty.

SM: You feel that the neoconservative course, as represented by the Reagan revolution, the Thatcher revolution or whatever similar revolutions there are in other capitalist countries, is not a really substantial change in the operation of modern capitalism. You believe that different changes are called for. Do I understand you correctly?

JKG: Yes, you do. An understanding of capitalism requires that we accept the fact of recurrent aberrations in public policy, and I regard supply-side economics and monetarism as such aberrations, ones which experience and good sense will reverse and are even now reversing.

SM: I am somewhat concerned at that particular conclusion. I feel that these aren't simple aberrations. Rather, they should be seen in the light of the emergence of the military-industrial complex, the transnational corporations and of very conservative forces inside modern capitalism that are trying to reverse the tide of the Keynesian reforms we have talked about before. What Keynes proposed was really aimed at making the capitalist system operate in a better, more efficient, more humane way. Perhaps the reforms you will be suggesting in a moment — again, the Galbraith reforms — go more along those lines.

JKG: Let's talk about what should be done. First, I would make the general but essential point that modern capitalism already produces or can produce enough goods. We don't suffer from an insufficiency of production.

In the recession-depression of the early eighties in the United States, we didn't miss the goods that weren't produced. There was no comment on that. We did, however, seriously miss the income and employment that weren't supplied. So I see as the central problem of present-day capitalism not the production of goods or the production of services — those can be accomplished. The central problem is the assurance of a secure flow of income to all the participants in the system.

I might add one further word here. We have always been in error in our tendency to measure progress by the increase in the gross national product. I would like to see progress measured by the number of people who have a full, secure role in the society.

SM: I couldn't agree with you more. I feel that in our own country and in other socialist countries, when the point is reached in economic development that the needs of the population for necessary products and services are satisfied, the main aim of the system should then be an increase in the quality of those goods and services and the quality of life in general. I think that this is more and more accepted in the capitalist world as well.

JKG: Yes, but I would go on in our case to two further points. Like all good Americans, I accord only grudging compliments to socialist achievement, but we have two problems that you don't have, problems we must solve.

First, especially in our big cities, we have far too many people without employment, without income, people who are, as indeed we now call them, the underclass. That I see as our greatest problem.

Second, if we examine the larger framework, we have far too great an inequality in the distribution of income. And, unfortunately, that hasn't been improving in these last years; on the contrary, it has been getting worse. Far too much of our total income goes to a minuscule fraction of the people at the top of the income ladder and far too little goes to those in the middle-income bracket and at the bottom.

SM: Would you be a little more specific in describing the kind of measures you think would be necessary to improve these aspects of modern capitalism?

JKG: You're right to ask. It's much easier to point out the problem than it is to say just how it should be solved.

I would, first of all, put major emphasis on strengthening our social and welfare programs so that there is a secure income for people who don't have employment. I have in mind women who are raising families, families with dependent children, the physically or mentally handicapped. There must be a mitigation of hardship there. I would also have very strong retraining programs for displaced workers. And I would spend a great deal more on good primary and secondary education. There is one generalization that can be made worldwide: there are very few well-educated people who are poor, and there are almost no poorly educated or illiterate people who aren't poor.

SM: But you would agree that there are some very poorly educated people who are, in fact, quite rich?

JKG: I am willing, reluctantly, to yield the point. In fifty years of teaching at Harvard, I have encountered some even there.

SM: It sounds as if in America welfare now consists of a set of measures aimed at the unfortunate, the people who don't have employment, the people who are disabled and so forth. Even the word "welfare" is different in connotation from unemployment compensation of a more temporary character. Wouldn't you feel that the social programs you are talking about — the welfare programs — should be aimed not only at the people who are in that condition but also at a larger part of the population? I have in mind those who are at work but who are, perhaps, in need of things that aren't available to them in the necessary amounts — better and lower-cost recreational facilities and other things, maybe even health services. Would you think that there should be development along those lines or do you think that will be taken care of by the market?

JKG: No, I don't think it will be taken care of by the market. Some thirty years ago, in a book, *The Affluent Society*, I held that our tendency is to private affluence and public squalor. I would continue to emphasize the importance of improvement in the public services that are needed by all but the very affluent. I have in mind primary and secondary education, which I mentioned a moment ago, recreation, libraries, clean streets, police services so that our streets are safe, and, of course, good medical care.

sm: Also public transportation, perhaps?

jkg: Public transportation and public housing. One of the curious facts of life is that the market system does not, in any industrial country, provide good inexpensive housing for the poor. It's one of the great defaults of capitalism.

On the other hand, there are some things we do very well, which in this era of self-criticism we should recognize. We provide extraordinarily good university education in this country; our state universities are superior institutions. And I am a great admirer of our public television system, something we don't talk about as much as we should. I do feel, however, that there is a great deal we still must do to ensure that our public affluence is on a par with our private affluence. One thing I didn't mention earlier is better environmental protection.

sm: Could we now turn to macroeconomic policy and see whether changes are needed there?

jkg: That is where most of my economics colleagues would begin, and I don't entirely deplore that. A great change is needed in that area, and it can be described very briefly.

We have been relying in these last years on monetary policy, high real interest rates and the magic of the Federal Reserve Board as a regulator of the economy and a safeguard against inflation. Just before you came here to Vermont, there was great excitement in the public press over who was to be the next head of the Federal Reserve. Mr. Volcker was replaced by Mr. Greenspan. It couldn't, in fact, have mattered less. We need to escape our fascination with monetary policy and the related assumption that capitalism can be guided and regulated by its magic.

sm: Aren't both of those people Wall Street figures, so it really didn't make that much difference anyway?

jkg: I am forced to agree with you; it didn't make any

difference. What is important is not a change in the leadership of the Federal Reserve but a change in macroeconomic policy. We must put a much greater reliance on fiscal policy and a much smaller reliance on monetary policy. In the simplest terms, we should now move to increase taxes, reduce the present budget deficit of the federal government and have much lower real interest rates. Lower interest costs, in turn, would encourage industrial investment and construction. This would be a stimulant to the economy and would lead to an improvement in our capital plant and housing.

To repeat: we have relied in these last years far too much on the presumed magic of monetary policy and far too little on the hard decisions of fiscal policy.

SM: What you're suggesting would be very unpopular. An increase in taxes would be something that would be frowned upon by the majority of the population as well as by the rich and the corporations. Higher taxation isn't a popular thing to advocate, and perhaps, realistically, it would be difficult to accomplish.

JKG: Far better to have higher taxes than higher interest rates as a controlling instrument in the economy. I haven't given up hope that long-run advantage will come to replace short-run preference.

SM: I couldn't agree with you more on the long-term advantage.

JKG: You're going to damage my reputation if you agree with me too much.

SM: But I always say that before I start contradicting you on something else. I believe that perhaps some increase in taxes would be necessary, but in the actual situation in the United States, as I've said, it would be a difficult thing to achieve.

I would think that perhaps more cutting of expenditure

would be called for instead. But since you have just been talking about expanding the welfare state, the cuts in expenditure couldn't come from that area; they would have to come from, say, military and defense spending.

JKG: I would hope very much that they might. This is the point to which I was coming. Let me say a word about it now. It's a matter on which I would particularly like to have the cooperation of the Soviet Union.

As matters now stand, a military initiative on your part encourages a military initiative on ours. You take some action, and that becomes the excuse for our initiating a new military expenditure, a new weapons development. We do something in the way of missiles, and you follow. It's an arrangement by which the military establishment on one side supports the military establishment on the other. And obviously it could lead to the ultimate nuclear debacle that we discussed earlier. It's also exceedingly damaging to the economic well-being of both countries.

SM: I think you may be correct as far as the recent past is concerned, but you're a little behind the times on these matters. The history of the last few decades has certainly been one of the armaments race. At this point I wouldn't think it would be useful to go into the question of who initiated what, who took the first step.

JKG: I was carefully avoiding that.

SM: Yes, it isn't productive. However, in the last two years under Mr. Gorbachev, I don't know of any military or weapons initiatives in the Soviet Union. I *do* know of initiatives on our part in the area of arms reduction, and these initiatives have to some extent been matched by the United States government. Therefore, I think there is hope. Let us come back later to the question of reducing military expenditures.

JKG: I find your statement most encouraging; I hope you find mine encouraging. If we don't succeed in persuading our readers on any other point, let us hope we persuade them — both our peoples — on the great mutual advantage in an escape from the arms race.

sm: Some people will, of course, argue that a cut in military expenditures will add to the economic difficulties of your country.

jkg: I have looked into that with great care, discussed it at length, and I don't believe it for a moment. Could I develop the point?

sm: If you would, it would be very helpful.

jkg: First, we have the inescapable fact that the great success stories of capitalism, perhaps the great economic success stories of the world since World War II, have been Japan and West Germany. Both are countries with relatively small military expenditures — in the case of Japan, minuscule military expenditures. Both have been able to use their skilled manpower and their capital resources to improve their civilian industries. The United States and Britain, on the other hand, have used much more of their manpower and their capital for arms.

And in the United States at the present time, as perhaps never before in our history, we have the pressure of public needs, some of which I have mentioned earlier. We have a deteriorating transportation system, a great lack of lower-cost housing, urgent urban deficiencies, increasing educational needs. So there are compelling public alternatives for the money we are now using for military expenditures.

sm: What you are saying is that the opportunity costs of a dollar spent for military expenditures have increased enormously. The latter are getting relatively far more expensive than at any time in the past.

jkg: Opportunity costs — the alternative reward forgone — is a fine old economic term; I'm glad to be reminded that I should use it.

SM: But not many people realize these enormous negative consequences of military expenditure.

JKG: I would say, on the contrary; that point is far more widely realized than people think. And it's becoming more thoroughly understood all the time. I think you're reflecting here a common inferiority complex. That is the tendency in the United States, as perhaps also in the Soviet Union, to assume that people who are wrong have somehow more moral force than people who are right.

SM: That reminds me to mention that there are people in the Soviet Union who still believe that military expenditure has a lot of spin-off into civilian industry, that it really produces large beneficial effects for the development of civilian technology. I always argue against that point; what is your attitude?

JKG: I argue against it too. There was a time in the past when there was some connection. The Boeing 747 was the spin-off of military development. Some satellite television came about in a similar way. But this is something that is egregiously exaggerated. I would particularly like to have somebody explain what beneficial civilian effect there is from the military expenditure on the very sizable conventional forces we both now maintain.

SM: I think there is no great spin-off there. I would understand it if the large numbers of soldiers in our armies were put to use in building roads or on other construction projects. That would be a very worthwhile and productive use of their time, but apparently they are rarely employed in those areas.

JKG: I would convert them into civilians paid at daily civilian rates rather than keeping them in uniform.

SM: We don't pay our soldiers as much as you do. But even as soldiers they could be profitably used in civilian construction.

Do you really think, however, that with the influential role your military-industrial complex has assumed in the last two or three decades, it is possible to curb its power and bring about a reduction in armaments expenditure — a reduction that would be beneficial to all?

JKG: I will ask you about the possibilities in the Soviet Union in just a minute. As far as the United States is concerned, I don't minimize the difficulty. However, when one gives up hope, one gives up all chance of accomplishing anything. And I have a feeling that the people of the United States are very strongly aware of this problem. In the presidential election next year all of the candidates — the Democratic candidates, at least — will be talking about the need for arms control and for restraint on military spending. This will be in response to very clearly articulated public opinion.

But tell me, how do you see the power of your military-industrial complex?

SM: In the last few years, especially since Mr. Gorbachev has become General Secretary of the Party, the role of the military in determining the country's policies, including the financial and economic policies, has been drastically reduced. The reforms that are now being implemented in the Soviet Union are all aimed at increasing civilian resources — the social sphere. It's obvious that you can't do this very successfully if you don't curb the resources going into the military sphere.

Also, in many cases, Mr. Gorbachev and the leadership of the Party have been instrumental in substantially changing our country's position on strategic and medium-range nuclear weapons. I think this has been done as the result of a considerable reduction in the influence of those who put an increase in arms at the forefront of national priorities.

Turning to a slightly different aspect of this problem, I understand that the amount of employment created by an additional dollar of your military expenditure has been on the decrease in recent decades. This shows the lessening effectiveness of military expenditure as far as stimulating the economy is concerned.

JKG: That's certainly true about employment. Military expenditure, particularly weapons expenditure, goes into relatively high salaries for technical specialists and into profits for the weapons firms. Only a relatively small part goes into general employment. Careful calculations have been made to this effect; all show that such expenditure is one of the least efficient ways of creating employment.

SM: It's also true that the material content of missiles is relatively much less than that of tanks or artillery. Less steel and other conventional materials are used per dollar of missile expenditure than is the case with expenditure for tanks. This means fewer jobs in the steel and other materials industries.

JKG: Old-fashioned guns and shells had a certain capacity to kill people too. I'm not greatly in favor of them either.

But, given our public needs, I don't believe that the transfer from military to civilian production in the United States would be a particularly difficult matter. What is the situation in the Soviet Union?

SM: In the Soviet Union there would be no difficulty at all in transferring from military to civilian industry. I indicated a little earlier that we are in a labor-deficient situation. Accordingly, any workers transferred from the military, either from the armed forces or from military industry, could be employed productively in civilian industries or services, which are always in need of expanding their resources of manpower.

JKG: There's an interesting related point here. As I said earlier, getting an increased production of goods is not our greatest urgency. It does, however, remain in some measure your greatest urgency — civilian goods, I mean.

SM: That's true, and it's why we're particularly interested in converting from military to civilian output. Reduction in military expenditure would also help to increase resources for expanding the public services, such as education, the medical services, recreational facilities, child-care facilities and so forth.

JKG: And there is another aspect to this that I would like to mention. It has been said in the past by some presumably responsible people in the United States that if we spend enough on arms, we can force your country into some kind of a compromise on arms control. I always doubted it. In both the United States and the Soviet Union the production of weapons and the management of a military establishment are an exercise in planned economy, are they not?

SM: All parts of our economy are more or less planned.

JKG: So our military establishment is competing with the Soviet Union in running a planned sector of the economy, and this is an area where, presumably, you are more experienced than we are.

SM: Yes. But I think your administration's basic idea has been to try to make us deploy more resources into the military and spend less on increasing the efficiency of our economy. I'm not sure that it isn't a self-defeating proposition. In recent decades we have seen that the Soviet Union, though technologically backward in many civilian areas as compared to the United States, has been able to keep up in the military field.

JKG: I am more than prepared to agree. My question remains, should we expect to compete, given your experience in economic planning?

SM: I would perhaps be in favor of a little more planning in the United States if it is for civilian purposes.

JKG: Now let me go on to a different matter: one of the legacies of the Keynesian revolution in the capitalist world is the tendency to look at all economic policy in macroecon-

omic terms — monetary policy, taxation, public expenditure. This has diverted attention from the substantial number
of reforms that are necessary in the microeconomic sector
of the economy, the market sector. Our discussion of needed
change wouldn't be complete without mention of these.

SM: Are you talking now about specific industries?

JKG: Yes. There is, first, the problem of our old or sick
industries. They are now much under discussion. We cannot
hope to prevent, and perhaps shouldn't try to prevent, a
substantial movement of our heavy industry or our textile
industry to the new countries. They need it, and the trend
is part of a long process. The newly industrialized countries
have the advantage here that was once ours. Perhaps we
may want to slow the process down on occasion, but I would
be opposed to any general resort to protection. Instead, our
policy should center on retraining and economic support
for our workers who become unemployed, something we
have already mentioned.

SM: But what does that mean in practical terms? You're
saying that you're in favor of supporting workers who would
lose their jobs because of the removal of the sick industries,
but you wouldn't support an attempt to modernize those
sick industries?

JKG: I wouldn't rule that out. But I don't think we are
ever going to modernize our steel industry or our shipbuilding industry. We won't be prominent in those industries
again; I think they are going or gone for good.

SM: Aren't we actually saying here that there is an attempt
to move heavy industries — what are sometimes referred to
as "dirty" air- or water-polluting industries — to the countries with lower wages so that they can benefit from the
development of those industries, while the more industrialized countries will benefit from the cheaper steel and other
products thus produced? Wouldn't this be a new form of
international exploitation? Some of the older industrialized

countries seem to be using for their own particular interests the desire of the developing countries to achieve full employment.

JKG: No, you old-fashioned Bolshevists, or should I say new-fashioned Bolshevists, are too sensitive to the issue of exploitation.

SM: Yes, we are always sensitive to exploitation whenever we see there is a danger of its existence or increase.

JKG: The Japanese, the Koreans and Taiwanese, the Indians all want these industries. And their people want to work in industrial plants, want to escape from the greater miseries of agricultural peasant life. For them industrialization is the dawn of a new existence. I would cite Marx to you; he said in *The Communist Manifesto* that one of the great achievements of capitalism was that it rescued people from what he called the idiocy of rural life. I am shocked that you are taking an anti-Marxist position on industrialization.

SM: What I am shocked at is that you're trying to dispose of what you don't need in your own country by moving it to others. Wouldn't it be a good idea if, instead, you exported your newly developing electronic industries, the "clean" industries, to the new countries and retained the traditional "dirty" industries? You could modernize them with the help of new technologies so that pollution was reduced.

JKG: In the first place, we're not capable of such a mammoth exercise in planned economy. Second, I wouldn't be in favor of the effort it would require even if it were possible. And I would add that the speed with which our electronic innovations pass to Japan, Korea and Taiwan is already one of the marvels of the age and something that causes great distress to our industries here.

SM: I know that. I know also that many of the electronic industries that end up in the newly industrialized countries are plants set up by transnational corporations, and quite a number of them are, in fact, working under subcontract to American military firms. That's true.

JKG: Obviously I can't get you away from your transnational corporations.

SM: No. I feel that modern capitalism is a transnational capitalism; in fact, I'm sure it is.

JKG: I think perhaps I was responsible for the use of the word "transnational." They were once called multinational corporations. I thought that dubious English, and I started calling them transnational corporations. Clearly I have my major convert in you.

SM: They are still called multinationals in the United Kingdom; I am using "transnational" because that's what's used in the United States.

But let's go on to some of the other American industries. Isn't it true that you also have a major problem of overproduction in agriculture?

JKG: This we must accept. It's one of the basic tendencies of the system, a tendency that can be traced to two circumstances.

One is the enormous productivity gains that have occurred in agriculture. We are talking today in a county in southern Vermont. There are only a few dairy farms left here, maybe a dozen or so major ones at the outside, and they probably produce as much milk with a handful of people as fifty or a hundred dairy farms did seventy-five years ago. And the same is true for all farm crops and products.

The other circumstance is that in agriculture no individual farm, however large, controls or even influences the supply. It's a pure competitive situation as compared with the oligopoly and implicit control of prices that exist in, say, the automobile industry.

SM: Oligopoly is just another one of the words you would rather use than, say, monopoly?

JKG: No, there is some technical difference — an oligo-

poly is a small number of sellers instead of a single mono-
polist — but I'm not going to quarrel about the minutiae of
economic theory.

It is necessary, inescapable, that we come to have some
public system of controlling supply in our agricultural system. Preferably it should be in conjunction with the other
similarly situated agricultural countries — Argentina, Canada, Australia and New Zealand. We are lagging badly on
this matter. There is now legislation before the Congress on
it, but the political situation is still far from favorable. Instead
of managing supply, we're paying enormous sums in subsidies to compensate for the low prices resulting from the
overproduction.

SM: Why is it that with all the high productivity in American agriculture, the costs of producing agricultural products are still so high and there have to be subsidies from the
government, especially as far as exports are concerned?

JKG: Our overproduction regularly brings prices below
costs. In addition, there have been some special circumstances in these last years. In the 1970s, we had a rather severe
run-up in agricultural land prices and heavy land purchases
at the higher prices. That left a lot of American farmers
with high indebtedness, high interest rates to pay on mort-
gages. However, the larger situation is that the competitive
market, the free market, results in overproduction, and
overproduction regularly brings farm prices below costs.

SM: The costs themselves should be very minimal. You
have indicated that there are enormous increases in your
agricultural productivity, which means you really don't em-
ploy that much labor in agriculture. You yourself have identified higher wage claims as one of the causes of the inflation
in industrial prices, but there is practically no labor used in
agriculture, and costs are still increasing. Is it the result of
the high administered prices of the commodities bought by
the farmers?

JKG: On machinery, fertilizer and the like there are administered prices. And they can be high, there's no question about that. But I wouldn't put too much emphasis on it.

The basic tendency in agriculture is for production to press prices down below costs. That's something we now offset, as I've said before, with subsidies. We must, however, deal properly with the problem by managing supply.

SM: If you compare the cost of producing milk and wheat in the United States with the cost of producing the same amount of milk and wheat in a developing country, your costs should be less since you are a more productive economy in a more productive system. But it turns out that the prices of your commodities in the world market are below what your costs are. I can't really understand how this happens. It would be interesting to know what you think about it.

JKG: I don't have the figures in mind. But the main point is the one I've already made: whether our costs are high or low, we have a resolute tendency to produce at levels that drive prices below costs.

SM: Let's go on to a different area. We have been talking about the increase in corporate bureaucracy and also, for that matter, government bureaucracy in the capitalist countries. Do you have any prescription that would help solve that problem?

JKG: Right here there is a convergence between developed capitalism and developed socialism — we both talk about bureaucracy and its problems. However, after we recognize that the bureaucracy ages and changes just as individuals do, I think we have to admit that there's no conceivable alternative to the modern large bureaucratic enterprise at the moment.

SM: What you're actually saying is that you don't have any prescription in that particular area.

JKG: You put the matter succinctly but accurately. Let me put the question back to you. You struggle much harder with the problem of bureaucracy in the Soviet Union than we do because you have the united mass of both the industrial enterprises and the state. Do you see an easy way to prevent an increase in bureaucracy in your case?

SM: No, I don't, and I think it's going to be one of the major factors that will affect the future of socialism.

I would be curious as to your ideas about whether the reforms you have suggested — the so-called Galbraith reforms — will, in fact, be achieved in the next, say, two decades. What is your general belief about how capitalism is going to develop in these coming years? What is your forecast of the immediate future? We know your prescriptions and your answers to the present problems. Now, what do you think is ahead as far as capitalism is concerned?

JKG: That's a good question on which to end today's discussion. I propose that next time we consider first my view of the future of capitalism and later we will hear your view of the future of socialism.

9

The Future of Capitalism

SM: Let's talk a little about the future of capitalism. Could you say a few words about the possibility of a deep crisis in the capitalist economies? It is claimed that extensive speculation on Wall Street and other stock exchanges around the capitalist world has led to a situation reminiscent of 1929. That was the eve of the last great depression. Are we in for a new Great Crash?

JKG: I approve of your mention of the Great Crash. That was the name of a book that I wrote some thirty-five years ago. If I might digress, it taught me an important lesson about book titles. I once asked in an airport if they were carrying copies of *The Great Crash*. The saleswoman looked at me with deep sympathy and said, "That certainly isn't a title you could sell here."

SM: Although it did sell well in other places.

JKG: It sold well or at least adequately in other places. No author ever thinks his book sells as well as it should.

But to answer your question: we have a small cottage industry in the United States that regularly turns out books warning of the next economic catastrophe. I have always been a little suspicious of them. However, as we sit here in the late summer of 1987, there is major speculation on Wall Street, and also on the Japanese securities markets. And we have much of what we have come to call corporate paper shuffling: mergers and acquisitions and the development of new instruments of finance, including one that bears the extraordinary name "junk bonds."

We know two important things about this activity. First, it doesn't contribute anything to the efficiency of industrial production in our system. It's an exercise undertaken by young men who have become experts in buying and recombining the assets of corporations. They do this not to improve the performance of those corporations but, alas, to make themselves more money. And they are making quite a bit.

Second, this activity loads our system with a great structure of debt. In the next episode of inflation, the Federal Reserve will increase interest rates and tighten credit. That could produce a severe crunch; there could be bankruptcies and other most disagreeable results.

I'm not, however, making that as a prediction. I warn you that when economists in the capitalist world make predictions, it's not because we know but because we are asked.

SM: What about the suggested reforms in the banking community, combining once again investment banks and commercial banks, entities that have been separated since 1933? This separation was the result, as I recall, of the Glass-Steagall Act, which was one of the first Roosevelt reforms.

JKG: I am always impressed by the way you remember the details of your early instruction on the American economy. On balance, I would be strongly opposed to the repeal of the Glass-Steagall Act because it would put the commercial banks into highly speculative investment banking operations. Some would conduct themselves in a respectable fashion; others would behave in an exceedingly dangerous way. The Glass-Steagall Act was one of several regulations that came after the fact of the great speculation of the 1920s, after the damage was done. It should not be repealed.

sm: Let's change direction a little bit now that we have talked about the possibility of a crash in the stock market and a deeper recession in the economy. Let me raise a different issue.

Throughout Europe, and I'm now talking about Western Europe, there is a new concept under discussion in what I would call neoconservative circles. That is the concept of the one-third/two-thirds society.

The one-third is what they consider the old-fashioned proletariat: low-wage workers but also people who are unemployed and old people on pensions, all of whom don't have a stake in the continuation of capitalism. The two-thirds either already have such a stake or can be led to have a larger one by selling them stocks, shares in government business enterprises or, as in Britain, municipally owned dwellings, and by other methods. This is claimed to be the basis for a radical turn away from the kind of Keynesian and Rooseveltian capitalism that has existed in the last fifty years and toward a new kind of capitalism, a *pure* capitalism without any kind of reform, without social democracy for that matter, without the welfare state and so forth. What would you think about this theory of the underclass and whatever comes with it?

jkg: A remarkable exercise of imagination, which should remain wholly in the area of imagination. One of the principal intellectual occupations of conservatives and their brethren, the neoconservatives, is to try to escape by one fashionable device or another from responsibility for the welfare of the poor.

I adhere resolutely to the notion that we must continue

a strong public responsibility for the least fortunate of our people. This, in fact, is the more conservative course. It reduces or eliminates the alienation that was so common in the last century and the early part of the present one. We certainly shouldn't destroy the structure of the welfare state for any theoretical nonsense of this sort, nor do I think we will. I think the common sense of the people of the industrial countries is sufficient to ensure that this won't happen.

sm: But you do accept the proposition that there is a so-called underclass?

jkg: I accept the proposition that in the United States and the other industrial countries we have people who don't have full access to the benefits of the system. I see them as the necessary recipients of public assistance — public education, public housing, public recreation, public libraries. This would not only raise their standard of living but ensure their future full participation in the economy.

Now, that having been said, let me add that in the last half century — in my working lifetime — we have made enormous progress in reducing the size of the underclass. We must, of course, keep on with that effort.

sm: Isn't that in some way the same thing the conservatives are saying: you are gradually reducing the underclass and laying the basis for a more conservative society?

jkg: It may well be that a society where everybody is happy and comfortable will be more conservative; I would be willing to run that risk. The conservatives are saying that this will come about by some marvelous exercise of laissez-faire; I am saying that the solution of the problem remains a major responsibility of the government.

sm: Now I see the difference between your approach and the conservative approach.

jkg: I am delighted.

sm: And I also see that you believe that the reforms leading to a better life for what is called the underclass are one of the needed movements of change within the capitalist system. Is that the way you view it?

JKG: Absolutely. You put it better than I do.

SM: Then perhaps we can go on to another subject. You have talked about the rise in the power of the corporate bureaucracy in society and the possibility of reforming the corporation. You said that you don't see a great possibility of doing the latter, but what about the possibility of limiting the former? I mean having less monopoly, fewer administered prices and less of what you call ossification. And, in the political sphere, weakening the political influence of the bureaucracy. Is it possible to reduce corporate power or change it?

JKG: Corporate power exists, there's no question about that. But, on the whole, I'm less concerned about it than I was when I first studied economics some fifty or sixty years ago. Then the power of the corporation was strongly manifested in its control of prices, in its influence on the labor market and in its pervasive presence in Washington. I think that, in general, that power has diminished in the last half century. The transfer of the corporation from the control of the old-fashioned capitalist to that of the manager has been one factor. And there is the lessening of monopoly power in the United States that has resulted from the invasion of the Japanese, Korean and Taiwanese producers. We have much more competition in the system today than we had a quarter of a century ago when I was writing *The New Industrial State*.

So, in trying to decide what I should worry about, I'm now putting my worries about corporate power on a rather secondary level.

SM: But you will concede that the corporate bureaucracy does resist the new attempts at reform?

JKG: I have argued that that is one of the points of greatest convergence between the United States and the Soviet Union.

sm: Would you feel, then, that reducing the power of the corporate bureaucracy in society would help the economic and social development of capitalism?

jkg: I suppose it would, but I don't see any way of doing it.

sm: Doing what?

jkg: Reducing the power of the corporate bureaucracy.

sm: This, you feel, isn't a realistic possibility?

jkg: I have to say that as far as the bureaucratic apparatus in the corporation is concerned, all we can do is to recognize its existence. And that it will continue to exist.

sm: A Democratic administration instead of a Republican one wouldn't change anything?

jkg: Absolutely not.

sm: There would still be a great corporate bureaucracy in ultimate control?

jkg: There would probably be some diminution of corporate political power in Washington, and as a Democrat I think that would be a good thing.

sm: There wouldn't be a diminution in the economic power of the corporation?

jkg: Its power in the economy wouldn't be changed one bit.

sm: There is another subject you have raised before, and that is the continuing change in both the class structure of American society, which we have partly discussed already, and the economic structure. By that I mean that there is a movement from a predominantly production-oriented economy to a predominantly service-oriented economy.

Do you feel there is a realistic possibility that the United States can survive in the world as a service economy, one that imports goods produced by other countries and sells its services to the rest of the world? Isn't there already a large trade deficit, a balance of payments deficit? Doesn't the movement to a service economy bring an aggravation of that problem?

jkg: I would, as I said earlier, move to control our budget deficit, lower interest rates and take other steps that would improve our trade deficit. But I leave that aside.

Can we survive as a service economy? No doubt for some people, many people, that would mean a lower standard of living. As we lose steel production, automobile production, chemical production and production of electronic gear and television sets to the Japanese and the Koreans, workers who are in relatively high-wage industries will have to go to work at very much lower wages for McDonald's — you know McDonald's?

sm: I do.

jkg: And very often their wives will have to go to work too. This can be a painful transition; I don't minimize its social effects and costs. But to answer your question, all production isn't steel or shipbuilding. As I've said before, when people are sufficiently supplied with things that work, they want better designs. And television or other enjoyments. So it's natural that in the United States we should move into the world of entertainment and the arts and, of course — something that has been more than adequately emphasized — into the world of higher technology. Also the world of education. As I've already observed, we still attract people from all over the world to our universities.

sm: You see the United States in the future as a society that will be entertaining itself, educating the rest of the world and doing a lot of very pleasant things while the other countries toil and produce the products of heavy industry for its consumption?

jkg: You put that in a rather prejudicial way, but I'm not going to quarrel with it too much.

You have been pressing me on the future of capitalism, and I'm not sure we have completely resolved it, so let me now press you on how you see its future.

sm: The capitalist economy is certainly now at the begin-

ning of a new technological revolution, and this revolution
may bring a general upturn instead of the current stagnation
or period of slow growth. However, I feel there are two significant barriers to this possibility.

One is the continuation of the arms race, which we have
discussed a number of times. I believe that the fruits of the
technological revolution should be more available to the consumer and less directed to military needs. After all, two
thirds of the gross national product of any economy goes to
consumer goods and services, and these still remain expensive in the capitalist world in spite of the great progress in
technology.

We were talking earlier about the high prices of agricultural products. Isn't it a shame that a carton of cigarettes
now costs as much as a good everyday watch?

JKG: Certainly not. It's merely that we've had a great
technological change in the production of timepieces. My
Harvard colleague David Landes has written a brilliant book
called *Revolution in Time* in which he points out that every
American now carries a watch that's far more accurate than
he or she needs. However, I don't deplore the fact that such
watches are relatively inexpensive. Not at all. You're making
a molehill out of a molehill.

SM: But isn't it true that if the technological revolution
were concentrated more on consumer goods and the tech-
niques of their production, it would be much easier to achieve
an upturn in the capitalist economy than if the present situation continues in which a very large part of new technical
innovation goes into weapons, space weaponry and the armaments race? That's what I'm talking about.

JKG: With that I agree. No, I was confining myself to your
limited case of cigarettes costing more than watches.

SM: Well, if you try to put me on the spot and say that
I'm promoting cigarette smoking, you're completely mis-
taken.

The other barrier that I think should be removed in order to have an improvement in the capitalist economies is the currently partially closed markets of the Third World. The large debt of the developing countries has been considerably reducing the amount of productive interchange between them and the industrial world in recent years.

JKG: I'm ashamed that I didn't mention that. It's very important.

SM: Recently there has been quite an interesting proposition put forward by the American author Peter Drucker, of whom you are probably aware. He has been writing about the economic disengagement of the leading industrial countries and the Third World in terms of raw materials and other commodities.

JKG: Please make that more specific; I don't understand.

SM: What he is saying is that the industrial countries are now less dependent on the Third World for the raw materials it used to supply in large quantities, and that has led to the relative decline in the prices of those raw materials and of the commodities produced by the Third World in general. This has brought about a large current balance of payments deficit for the developing countries. And a large increase in Third World debt. Let me add that if this debt were done away with, the enormous potential markets of the Third World would be opened up to products and services from the industrialized countries. That would be a major factor in supporting an upturn in the world economy.

JKG: I would agree, but I would put it in a little less dramatic terms. We are not going to see those Third World debts repaid.

I hope that all people in the socialist world understand the terminology of debt as it has recently developed. Now when a debt isn't paid, the country involved doesn't go into default. The debt is "rolled over." Having been rolled over and still being unpaid, it is "rescheduled"; then having been rescheduled and still being unpaid, it is called "a problem loan"; a problem loan that isn't repaid is then called a "non-performing asset."

Those are the new semantics. My own view is, as I've said before, that these nonperforming loans will never be repaid. The sooner we clean up the situation, come to terms with the fact of default, accept the loss, the better it will be.

Let me say just one further word, which, you will be happy to know, will be in further agreement with you. Once we have accepted the reality that these debts are not going to be paid, the debtor countries, which are now struggling to come up with interest payments and are having austerity forced on them by the International Monetary Fund at some danger to democratic government, will be able to buy more goods from the developed industrial countries. That, in a modest way, supports your proposition and Drucker's that our policy toward the Third World can have a positive effect on the economies of the developed countries.

sm: In trying to sum up, I want to say that, in general, the socialist world is interested in the improvement of economic conditions in both the industrialized countries and the Third World, and it isn't at all interested in the economic collapse of capitalism.

We feel that the current stagnation is breeding a lot of additional conflict and creating a situation in which there is a drive to produce more armaments as a possible way to stimulate the economies. The better the economic conditions in the world, the better the basis for more normal political relations between capitalism and socialism.

jkg: I accept that, but there is one other point on which I would like to register a view. I would like to see both the capitalist and the socialist countries sell fewer arms to the Third World. This is one of the disgraceful facts of our time. People who don't have enough to eat see their governments spending large sums of money for highly sophisticated weapons, which they don't need and, in some cases, are incapable of using.

sm: You see now that the market mechanism isn't ideal; there is demand for some products that shouldn't really be satisfied.

jkg: If we agree to stop selling arms to Pakistan, will you stop selling arms to India?

sm: I think that's a good proposition; it might be possible.

jkg: It's something we should negotiate.

sm: Negotiations on the subject of limiting arms sales to the Third World countries have, in fact, been going on for a number of years, and, for reasons that are obvious, they haven't been too successful, but I believe in the future this will have to happen.

We should think of the future of the Third World as well, because by selling arms to the developing countries, we are promoting their militarization. We should, instead, cooperate in promoting their economic and social development and the improvement of their standard of living; that's where our energies should be directed.

jkg: I agree.

Now that we've resolved the future of capitalism, may I add that I'm pleased to hear you say that our well-being in the capitalist countries is not damaging to the socialist world, that prosperity and peace can go together. That is definitely something on which we can agree.

10

The Future of Socialism

JKG: We come now to the future of socialism. How do you see that future and how do you see the development of the Gorbachev reforms?

SM: I see three possible scenarios. Of course, these are more or less simplified, and life can be more complicated. What may actually happen may be a combination of the possibilities I will suggest.

JKG: Let us agree that economists make something complicated partly because it is complicated, partly to show that they have a deeper understanding than that of the public at large. I countenance simple statements.

SM: The first scenario is based on the danger of bureaucratic sabotage of the current antibureaucratic reforms, and this is a scenario that would mean a continuation of the status quo.

Why is this a possibility? First of all, one should realize that the current reforms are not going to bring about economic prosperity by magic. Turning to a new system is fairly difficult. When conditions of an expanded market mechanism have been established, the enterprises will find it hard at first to find customers or markets for their products or the sources of the raw materials and machinery they need for their production. There may be other problems, and all this may even lead temporarily to some stagnation in the economy or lower growth rates. So, at the same time that the country has initiated a program of trying to accelerate the economy, what the bureaucracy will see is the new system seeming to decelerate the economy. They will press for a return to continuous day-to-day interference in, and control of, the affairs of the enterprises. Something like that occurred in 1964, when Khrushchev was accused of destroying central planning. It may happen again. The bureaucracy and the shadow economy circles are already trying hard to prove that the new system cannot work. They even go to the extent of artificially creating new deficits in the economy, particularly in the supply of consumer goods.

JKG: This would seem to be related to the fact that the people who comprise the bureaucracy are generally well satisfied with their positions.

SM: They are satisfied with the old system, and they aren't willing to adjust to the new situation. Adjustment for a great number of them may, indeed, be very painful. Some may be (and already are being) transferred to the productive enterprises, and they will feel they have lost the prestige and power associated with their former jobs. However, I think you won't be surprised, Professor Galbraith, by the ability of a bureaucracy to adjust to new circumstances, to find new reasons for, and new forms of, its own existence.

Look at the Hungarians, for example. Hungary is a country where, for all practical purposes, central planning has now been discontinued for a number of years, where the centralized bureaucracy has presumably been stripped of a lot of its power. But, as indicated by the very eminent Hungarian economist Janos Kornai in a recent article, "the old command system of direct bureaucratic control in Hungary" has been transformed into a system of "indirect bureaucratic control." So there is a new kind of control, a new kind of bureaucracy.

JKG: That's very interesting, and I'm particularly pleased by the reference to Professor Kornai, who is my colleague at Harvard. He teaches half the year in Cambridge and half the year in Budapest. A very good example of socialist and capitalist convergence, wouldn't you say?

SM: Some people say that Yugoslavia was successful in eliminating the centralized bureaucracy, but there is a lot of talk now of the regional and local bureaucracies interfering in the affairs of the producing enterprises there.

To sum up: the results of the first scenario, of the bureaucracy remaining in control in the socialist countries, would be continuing economic stagnation; inflation, in some cases runaway inflation, as in Yugoslavia; high foreign indebtedness, as in Poland; and other features that we don't want to see perpetuated. So the first scenario isn't really one that will be favorable for the continued existence of socialism. Even in our country there are people who are trying to use the reforms to increase prices drastically across the board. This is very dangerous and harmful.

JKG: Let's go on to the second scenario, but at a later stage I want to ask you, where in the Soviet Union does Mr. Gorbachev get his support against the bureaucracy?

SM: I think we should deal with that right now. He has support from the Party; from a large part of the population, particularly the workers in the enterprises; from the farmers who need more freedom to run their farms; and much support from the intelligentsia, especially the creative intelligentsia, by which I mean the literary and artistic world, the press, the media in general.

JKG: People like ourselves?

SM: The academic people and writers, if you wish.

JKG: You passed over that compliment very quickly.

sm: I would say it's not so much the economists who are now in the forefront of the fight against bureaucracy, although they have done something in that area. It is, rather, the literary world, the journalists. *The Literary Gazette,* for example, has been producing very deep and wide-ranging criticisms of the operation of the bureaucracy in various fields, economic, political and judicial. So I think that is where Mr. Gorbachev is getting his support.

The second scenario is a completely different possibility, and that is a movement toward a more complete market socialism. This doesn't mean reestablishing the capitalist system, although it would involve a much wider exercise of private initiative and private entrepreneurship. What it would principally mean is leaving price determination completely to the market, as you suggested when we were discussing the economic reforms. And a free labor market would be introduced. There would be more flexibility in wage determination and a flexible capital and credit market within the system. What it would amount to is socialism with a total absence of central planning.

jkg: This would be something on the present Hungarian model?

sm: Not really, because, as Kornai said, the current situation in Hungary is indirect bureaucratic control rather than a completely liberalized market system. The latter may be the direction in which Hungary is headed, but a better example of what I mean is really Yugoslavia, where there is no centralized planning at all. There is, as I've said, some interference from local authorities but no centralized planning.

jkg: I don't sense that you are totally enthusiastic about this scenario. What would you see as its difficulties?

sm: I've already mentioned the possibility of runaway inflation under these circumstances. This involves a concept you yourself have put forward in your books — the idea of countervailing power. In a socialist market system, where workers' collectives presumably would be in charge of the enterprises, there would be no countervailing power to prevent an uncontrolled increase of their money incomes and prices. I'm talking now about the countervailing power in the relations between management and labor, between the enterprises and the central authorities. I suspect that without it there would be runaway inflation. That's one difficulty I see in the second scenario.

jkg: Putting it in slightly different terms, there would be nothing to control the increase in workers' wages and the pressure of those wages on the market?

sm: Exactly. In the capitalist system, whatever you may think about it, the management of the corporations or the capitalists themselves act as a brake on the demands of the workers. I'm all for the workers getting a fair share, but I'm not in favor of a continuous increase in wages beyond productivity gains, and that's exactly what has been happening in Yugoslavia.

jkg: In my original discussion of countervailing power, I argued that the worker, the trade union, the cooperative, even the chain store or supermarket, all come to develop power that offsets that of the producing corporation. What we would have here in the socialist countries is power residing in the workers' cooperatives and no offsetting restraint on the part of the employer.

sm: Or for that matter on the part of a central planning authority. Suppose, however, that this weakness could be overcome. Suppose that the market within a complete market socialism operated efficiently enough and there was no runaway inflation. What reason have we to think that such a socialist system would operate better than the capitalist system, which has an even more complete market mechanism?

jkg: A complete market socialism, I take it, is somewhat

beyond the range of current possibility and imagination.

sm: It may be so, but suppose the question does arise. Why not have the capitalist system as it is and not just something that is masquerading as a market system?

jkg: The market socialism you are talking about is still far short of capitalism because it wouldn't involve the private ownership of productive property, would it?

sm: No, not on a large scale, but it would have some of the features of capitalism. For example, there would be considerable social inequality. Look at Hungary. I'm not criticizing the situation there, but a recent census showed that within that system, which is a limited market system, there is a small minority with very high, presumably legal incomes, and this minority comprises about one percent of the total population. This isn't very different from the pattern of income distribution in some capitalist countries.

jkg: That's very interesting. Now, what about the free labor market in the second scenario?

sm: What is a flexible labor market if not the possibility of unemployment and the use of employment to regulate the system? You have here again one way of creating a countervailing power as far as the incomes of the workers are concerned. But that's really going back to problems with which capitalism traditionally has had to cope. I can't understand why we should do it.

jkg: You are saying, why should socialism take on the social problems of capitalism?

sm: Exactly.

jkg: Now tell me about the third scenario.

sm: The third scenario is what I might call a true democratic centralism. What that means is a combination of the best features of central planning with the best and the least harmful features of the market, making good use of both.

Now, we know and we have reiterated a number of times that the market isn't necessarily a perfect tool. And neither price nor profit gives the enterprises, the producing firms, adequate information. Under socialism, central planning and centralized control may be used to correct and improve the operation of the market and solve some of the problems that are inevitably encountered when one tries to couple planning and the market.

Let's take the price system, for example. You have asked, why not a complete free price determination? I have answered that the price mechanism isn't perfect. Future planning needs more information than today's prices provide, and future prices are unknown. What the central planning authorities could do, in principle, is to estimate a system of future prices that would be totally consistent with the plan and with the general economic strategy of the country; methods already exist that can compute such future prices. The late, very well known Nobel Prize laureate Leonid Kantorovich of our country produced a number of studies that developed the methodology of computing what is generally known in the West as shadow prices. These are now called in our country the prices of optimal planning. Perhaps it's time to bring this methodology from the theoretical stage to a more practical one and have the planning authority use more of the available computations to guide the economy in the directions that are thus forecast and foreseen. That's one of the things that the central authorities could do.

JKG: I'm not entirely clear on this scenario. It involves some fairly difficult technical matters. You would accept the prices given by the market except under circumstances where, by long-range calculations, those prices could be improved and made socially or economically more acceptable. Am I right on that?

SM: I think you're basically right.

JKG: Give me a practical example of where the market price would be wrong and the calculated price right.

SM: If we turn, for example, to the price of oil twenty or

thirty years ago, it was fairly low, but it seemed from the point of view of the immediate market situation to be all right. However, it didn't take into account the fact that oil was more and more becoming a scarce commodity. If the planning authorities had looked ahead twenty years, they would have come to the conclusion that the future price of oil would, in fact, be higher.

JKG: Given that scenario today, you would raise the price now as a conservation measure?

SM: Yes, as a conservation measure but also as a measure that would reduce the undue reliance of the economy on a material that is thought to be cheap at the moment but will be expensive ten or twenty years hence. The technologies we are now using would not otherwise be adapted to a fuel that is becoming more expensive.

JKG: You might reduce the price of atomic energy to get it better established?

SM: Yes, possibly. It could be that prices may have to be higher initially for new products or technical innovations in order to promote the industries that provide them. Those industries may have to be subsidized so that the initial high costs are assumed by the state and not passed on to the consumer.

JKG: You would probably have a certain number of young Americans picketing the central planning authority if it thus favored atomic energy.

SM: Yes, I suppose we would.

JKG: I see the point, and there are some interesting possibilities here. You could raise the price of automobiles to keep down air pollution and traffic and keep low the price of mass transport in order to encourage people to use it.

SM: That has been done in the past. Actually, I believe that the price of cars is already far too high in our country. It could be somewhat lower, and we could have more cars with better antipollution devices. But as far as public transportation is concerned, I agree with you; I don't think it would be useful to set the prices in that area by the market. Even now there are efforts to raise them well above the actual current cost. The public — through the media — is fighting against those attempts.

JKG: So your third scenario would be a market economy except where it's undeniably clear that there would be social advantages from altering the price structure.

Now I have a further question. Doesn't a design like the one in Hungary continue a very substantial bureaucratic apparatus — as my Harvard colleague Professor Kornai has said?

SM: I don't think so, because price control of that kind wouldn't entail a lot of bureaucratic personnel. Most of the prices — and these would be really a limited number of basic prices — would be computed by electronic methods and not by hand, and it wouldn't involve a centralized setting of many prices.

JKG: I was, in my distant past, quite surprised at how many people it takes to fix prices. In 1941, I was put in charge of prices in the United States with six or seven people under me. I ended up with some thousands.

SM: But at that time you didn't have computers, and you weren't basing your price policy on a system of optimal prices. You were doing something else.

JKG: We were, in fact, controlling *all* prices. But I don't insist that my example is entirely relevant.

SM: I think we could have a small apparatus doing this today. But let me point to some of the other things that the central economic authorities should be in charge of under this scenario.

You realize that we have very little experience in operating a market economy. When I say we, I don't mean myself; I mean the management of the enterprises. So somebody has to educate the managers, set up a system that provides them with the necessary business education and promotes the ones who already have had some experience in the area. This, I think, would also entail teaching our managers about marketing in the West.

JKG: We must consider the possibility of bringing more of your people to the Harvard Business School.

SM: Yes, but I don't think you'd be able to educate all of them there. We do have a number of business schools now ourselves, although we should have more. However, the basic responsibility of the central authorities should be to find people who would be sufficiently independent, sufficiently capable of pursuing the future well-being of the enterprise, its workers and the industry as a whole. They shouldn't be people trained in the old bureaucratic way.

JKG: There are two or three further questions on which I would like to press you. What about the failing enterprise, the one that obviously doesn't make money but still continues? What do you do about that? Are you going to have our Chapter 11 bankruptcy laws?

SM: Actually, as I've said before, we do have a bankruptcy law or rather a provision included in our new law on enterprises. Such a possibility is considered, and the same is true in Yugoslavia, Hungary and China, where bankruptcy laws are now being experimented with.

JKG: Arrangements by which the enterprise is simply terminated?

SM: Yes, and workers are transferred to other jobs after some period of unemployment.

JKG: There will be a punitive period of unemployment?

SM: There will, but let me say a few words about that. I consider bankruptcy really an extreme contingency as a solution for the failing enterprise. You will agree that under your system bankruptcy isn't very much used nowadays, especially for large corporations. It used to be quite a wide-spread practice in early capitalism.

JKG: Yes. However, just today the *New York Times* had a full page devoted to the various notices concerning the bankruptcy of the LTV Corporation.

SM: I saw it. But under your bankruptcy laws the corporation isn't really closed out. It is usually reorganized in some way, either by the banks or by someone else.

What I am suggesting is going to happen in the Soviet Union is that the central economic authorities will have responsibility for organizing enterprises in the most efficient way. If they foresee that some area of industry is heading for long-term difficulties, they will take steps beforehand to help reorganize and modernize the plant or to change the character of its output.

JKG: I follow that, but it seems to me that every one of your remedies gets back to a central authority, doesn't it?

SM: It does, and that's what I'm trying to say. You see, the market may not show the enterprise that it's going to go bankrupt in three years, but the central authorities may, and they will have the responsibility to forecast those situations. In that case, they would need to have a contingency plan available for the enterprises that are failing.

JKG: I assume that those bureaucrats you so strongly condemned are still going to have a certain function. Every time something goes wrong, they come back into your picture.

SM: The central authorities will have to give the bankrupt or unprofitable enterprise substantial assistance in modernizing or changing its market orientation within the economy. That will be their function. The new kind of rational planning authority will think about reorienting the plant, modernizing it and finding a smooth way to adapt to the new situation.

The basic concern is that the workers of the plant should

not be unemployed because of the errors of the plant management or of the bureaucrats in the planning system. That's what I'm trying to say; it's the responsibility of the central authority to prevent bankruptcy or unemployment.

JKG: We said a moment ago that there would be a brief period of punitive unemployment. I gather that that punishment isn't going to be very severe.

SM: Such punitive unemployment is provided for, but it would occur only in extreme circumstances.

JKG: I understand.

I sensed on my earlier visits to the Soviet Union, and I have heard you yourself, among others, say, that in Soviet industry there is a major gap as between the technological innovations of the research institutes — the known technology of the Soviet Union, as well as of the West and Japan — and their application. Is that a problem, and how will it be solved?

SM: It is a problem. The socialist system, which was extremely responsive to technological change in, say, the thirties and forties, has become in many ways bureaucratic and slow in following and anticipating the basic directions of modern science and technology. And this applies not only to most ministries but also to the "leaders of science" — the State Committee for Science and Technology and the Academy of Sciences. In recent decades the Academy has followed the path of all increasingly large, poorly managed, inefficient institutions. Leadership has come in many cases from people who haven't excelled in any area of science, and they are inherently incapable of directing progress in that field or in technology.

I feel that it is now the task of the central authorities to see to it that science and its institutions are debureaucratized as soon as possible; otherwise there will be a serious lag in the system.

JKG: Again I have a question. Aren't you saying that the people who now have power in these institutes have power in the Academy and are going to be called on to reform themselves. Is that practical?

SM: No, I'm not saying that. Under the new system there is going to be an arrangement — and this is widely discussed in the scientific and academic community — by which the directors of the institutes will be elected by the members of the institutes on the basis of their scientific and academic qualifications rather than because of their bureaucratic ability.

JKG: They will be elected by the institute members rather than being appointed by the ministries?

SM: Yes, there will no longer be appointment by the ministries or by the top Presidium of the Academy of Sciences.

JKG: I find that very persuasive. But this isn't going to be a popular step with the old boys who get thrown out.

SM: It won't be at all, but it will have to happen. There has to be a change of blood in the organism.

JKG: Do say a few more words here about how the institutes and the Academy of Sciences now get Soviet innovations or those from the United States, Japan or elsewhere into actual use. And I would like to hear more specifically how that could be accomplished better.

SM: I suggest three things. First, we should utilize and learn from the experience of some of the more successful capitalist enterprises in the West, those where research and development — R & D as you call it — is directly connected with production and sales. There is already a good example of how this works in the German Democratic Republic. There the enterprises that combine R & D with production have been more successful in technological progress than their counterparts in the other socialist countries.

Point number two: in the early experience of the Soviet

Union in the thirties and forties, crash groups, particularly in the area of armaments and military technology, were organized to develop the appropriate new technology quickly. Where the need for technological progress seemed to be very acute, as in nuclear energy or space development, these crash groups were very successful.

JKG: We have that same tendency to excel in the more destructive aspects of human activity.

SM: I'm talking about outer space and peaceful exploits, not just military needs — about peaceful nuclear energy, not just the bomb.

JKG: One of the examples of that early success, I suppose, would be the notable flight of Mr. Gagarin.

SM: That's true. But there was also the first jet that flew transatlantic and trans-European flights — the famous Russian TU-104.

JKG: I rode in it, my first jet flight.

SM: It made a sensation in 1955 or 1956, when it was first operational. These are examples of crash programs, and there is now the possibility of setting up similar crash programs in various areas in which we're currently lagging.

JKG: I find that fascinating. When you stop and think of the development of the jet plane, the Sputnik and Mr. Gagarin's space flight, you remember how we thought of the Soviet Union as a leader in technology in those days. We don't do so now.

SM: The reason is that a country that was technologically backward in many other respects was then technologically very progressive in the particular areas that it managed to organize on a crash basis.

That is the second possibility for affecting change. The third possibility is using some of the experience of the United States and perhaps other countries in what is called risk capital. That means setting aside a reserve of capital and material resources that could be channeled to smaller units. These smaller units would be able to achieve faster results than the large industrial organizations, perhaps as cooperatives.

JKG: Earlier in our discussion there was some danger of confusing the Galbraith reforms with the reforms acceptable to the whole American republic. Are you now talking about Menshikov reforms or Gorbachev reforms, or are the two identical?

SM: I am talking about ideas that have been expressed by Mr. Gorbachev in his economic program of reforms, and I'm adding some concrete examples to the ideas he has suggested. But let's put it this way: whatever I'm discussing here is generally along the lines that are currently being advocated in the Soviet Union.

JKG: I have a final question on risk capital. According to orthodox economics, a higher price is usually involved to cover the risk. Will that higher price be part of your system?

SM: I believe there's nothing wrong with that; society should be ready to pay a higher price for risk, particularly if it results in technical progress.

I would like to summarize here and say that there are many areas in the microeconomy where socialism has to learn and learn fast from capitalism — from private enterprise, from the market. If it manages this, then, by combining the least harmful effects of the market and private enterprise with the advantages on the macroeconomic and social levels that are part of the planning system, we may be able to do better than capitalism. This is the scenario I prefer for the socialist society.

JKG: Thank you very much.

I suppose I might add one word of clarification. I assume we agree on our terminology. By microeconomics, we refer, essentially, to the behavior of the individual firm and market. This is distinct from macroeconomics, which is the overall behavior of the economy as influenced by fiscal, monetary or other broad government policy.

sm: Or, in our case, by the macroeconomic plan in the socialist system.

jkg: I thought such a word of reminder might be useful to those who have forgotten their early economics courses under Menshikov and Galbraith.

11

Economic and Political Relations Between the United States and the U.S.S.R.

JKG: There's one tendency in our economic and political relations that I have long considered unfortunate; I wonder if we're moving away from it. In the socialist-communist world it has always been assumed that capitalism doesn't work or is a passing phase. And there has been a well-articulated assumption in much of the capitalist world that socialism is a failure. Could we agree that both of them work far better than would have been imagined fifty or seventy years ago; that, in fact, they both are likely to survive, and survive even a considerable capacity for bad management? If so, this will call for a basic change in our attitudes.

SM: I believe the view that the other system works exceedingly badly is something of an ideological cliché that has been developed in certain parts of our two societies. I wouldn't think that businessmen — or, in our case, those who manage the economy and determine foreign policy — have taken it too seriously.

JKG: It's mentioned in your speeches and our presidential

press conferences, but it isn't something anybody much believes?

s M: That's right, at least in terms of practical policies.

I think you would agree that there was a great depression in the West in the 1930s, the deepest depression in the history of capitalism. Obviously your system wasn't working well then. But it was during this period that our trade and general relations with the United States, and for that matter with many other capitalist countries, expanded at a tremendous rate.

j k g: It was then that Roosevelt recognized the Soviet Union?

s M: In 1933, yes.

j k g: And we had a very admiring ambassador to your country — Joseph E. Davies?

s M: That's true. But those better relations started even before Roosevelt came to power, and rapid economic growth in the Soviet Union perhaps helped in the establishment or reestablishment of diplomatic relations between the two countries. I will tell you why. This was the period when we were pursuing a goal of rapid industrialization, and we had an enormous demand for imported machinery. In fact, at one point we imported forty percent of the total American exports of machinery. We were a good market for the capitalist system when it was in a time of great depression. Some might ask why we were helping capitalism, but in practical terms we were helping ourselves.

j k g: We would be glad to have that kind of help again any time.

s M: We will come back to that, I hope.

j k g: Let me ask the next obvious question. Can we agree that good economic performance is generally good for political relations between our two countries? To be specific, is there any reason why you should fear a better performance by capitalism or we should fear the success of the Gorbachev reforms?

I think myself we can both stand each other's success and should welcome it. Do you agree?

SM: I agree, but the historical record has been rather mixed. The Great Depression — your most unsuccessful economic period — brought us good relations with some capitalist countries. But economic depression also led to very dangerous tendencies, like the fascism of the 1930s. This, in turn, led to aggression and, eventually, to World War II.

JKG: That's certainly true and worth remembering.

SM: Some people would say that such adverse consequences were unique and would never be repeated, but I believe that times of recession or stagnation in the modern world tend to lead to the production of more armaments because to some people military expenditure seems a way out of the economic difficulties. And there's also a tendency to sell more arms to other countries at such times. Greater military output and larger military exports always result in bad international relations.

JKG: I wouldn't wholly disagree with that. However, I think we can put behind us the episode of fascism as it developed in the 1930s, first in Italy and then in a more extreme form in Germany. I don't see the possibility of a depression in the capitalist countries that would create that degree of political extremism and reaction. Nonetheless, the temptation to use military expenditure as a form of public works does, indeed, exist, so I would put the question back to you: Is there some danger in your country of using a period of economic stagnation as an excuse for greater military expenditure?

SM: I would think that perhaps we should look at this in a different way and talk about periods of reform, not of stagnation. Periods of reform in the Soviet Union have always been associated with an attempt to move our resources from military to civilian use. This was true of the years after Stalin's death in 1953, when there were the first attempts to improve relations between our two countries. And it was true again in the Kennedy period in the United States, which coincided with attempts at economic reform in the Soviet Union.

It's true now of the Gorbachev era, when you are seeing drastic changes in the priorities within our system. The Gorbachev reforms are trying to effect a much more peaceful policy, a policy aimed at gaining accord with the United States on such matters as nuclear arms. These things — reform and peaceful initiatives — come together in our country, I'm sure of that.

However, it doesn't follow of necessity that a period of stagnation leads to an attempt to spoil relations. It's clear that periods of bad relations only add to the economic problems of the socialist system.

JKG: This impresses me very much. You are saying that fundamental to reform in the Soviet Union is a shift from military to civilian resources. In any reform period this will be a central effort?

SM: I think that is also true of the capitalist system. The reforms you suggested yourself in one of our previous discussions are really contingent on some reduction in military expenditure. I'm referring to the expansion of the welfare state and related matters.

JKG: I think that's true, and it's a form of convergence I very much welcome.

SM: I, too, would welcome convergence in that area.

But to end this discussion of the military issue, let me just say that there seems to have been considerable correlation between periods of bad relations and the times when, for various reasons, plans were being made for long-term expansion in military output in both our countries. Take the build-up of strategic weapons in the late sixties and early seventies. Once that was over, there came détente. This was more or less accepted as a kind of pause between periods of intensive militarization.

JKG: Let me plead for some clarification on that; I have some difficulty understanding it. You are saying that we have episodes of military build-up, and during those periods, whether in the U.S.S.R. or the United States, there is a tendency to support the build-up by being disagreeable in international affairs?

SM: That's what happened in the late sixties and again in the early eighties, when there was a military build-up in the United States and also in the Soviet Union.

JKG: This is a form of convergence of which I don't approve.

SM: Absolutely not. We wouldn't support that kind of convergence either.

But I also worry about another issue. I have read a few statements by some of your politicians. For example, Richard Perle and others . . .

JKG: Richard Perle isn't a politician; he's a public bureaucrat.

SM: Call him whatever you wish, he still remains Richard Perle.

JKG: He's now writing novels. That's an occupation for him that I much recommend.

SM: Perhaps we should see it as a transformation from a military to a civilian use of his talents. However, I'm not particularly worried about Richard Perle himself, but there have been a few questions from people like him in the United States asking why the capitalist world should support the Gorbachev reforms when they're only helping socialism become stronger. I read a commentary in one of your newspapers, I think it was the *Christian Science Monitor*, that the better socialism becomes, the more attractive a choice it becomes in the eyes of the Third World. And then it may constitute a danger to American policies.

Do tell me your view on this matter. I will then add what I have in mind as to the situation in our country.

JKG: One extraordinary feature of American public life is that at any given time you can hear almost any opinion, including the views of Richard Perle.

However, I believe, and I think most Americans believe, that Soviet well-being is *not* dangerous to the United States. It brings tranquillity in your country just as our well-being does in ours. And this is in the interest of peace. In consequence, most of us very much want to see the Gorbachev reforms succeed. I would be categorical on that, and categorical as to the views of the majority of Americans on that.

As to the Third World countries, I don't believe it's a matter of their choosing between the two systems. As you know, I regard the development of the Third World as a process in which the possibility for socialism or communism comes very late. The ruling requirements for the early stages of economic development are a market economy, small-scale agriculture free of the domination of landlords and a strong emphasis on eliminating illiteracy. In these last years one of the major errors of public thought and policy in the United States — an error that is perhaps even more prevalent in the Soviet Union — is the belief that socialism is a possible model for a country that is just starting its economic development.

Conservation of scarce resources is essential for all social development. The scarcest resource in Sub-Sahara African countries is administrative capacity, and socialism, I think you would agree, places a far greater strain on administrative capacity and resources than the market economy does.

SM: You mean that the corporate bureaucracy wouldn't like to move to the Sahara or Sub-Sahara in Africa?

jkg: No, it wouldn't, except in pursuit of oil or other natural resources. Neither IBM nor socialism is relevant in Chad or Ethiopia.

sm: I would take exception to that proposition. I think perhaps in the future Chad may become one of the centers of technological progress in the world. I don't believe that the African countries are doomed to remain in the cellar of civilization forever.

jkg: I didn't say that; what I said was that they have to pass through an inevitable developmental stage in which the market economy comes first.

sm: That may be possible. Let me say that there is also . . .

jkg: I have your agreement on that, do I?

sm: I say that it's possible.

jkg: Sounds evasive to me, but I accept the evasion.

sm: There is no clear answer to that question; whether it's true or not has to be borne out by history.

But let me say that we do have people within the socialist system who would argue that in the world as a whole a scenario of economic growth and better economic performance under capitalism isn't something we should approve of or desire.

jkg: It delays the socialist revolution in, say, the United States?

sm: Yes, it delays the revolution in the capitalist countries, and it helps soften some of the contradictions of capitalism — both its internal contradictions and what we call the interimperialist rivalry between the United States, Western Europe and Japan. So there are people in the Soviet Union who would ask, why should we help capitalism?

jkg: I read a few weeks ago that your very distinguished countryman Yevgeny Yevtushenko said in an interview, "Your hard-liners help our hard-liners and our hard-liners help your hard-liners." They reinforce each other's image of danger and hostility, including the danger from the success of the other side.

sm: Let me quite seriously answer the specific observation of our hard-liners that we are helping capitalism. I am in general agreement with you as to the socialist model if used in the less developed and also in the most developed, industrialized countries of the world. The reason for that is obvious. I have already talked about it before: socialism hasn't been able up to now to show superiority over developed capitalism in productivity, in economic efficiency or, for that matter, in the level of living standards.

Now, with that in mind, I have to say that if socialism seriously wants to be a model for other people in the world, it has to be the most productive, the most efficient, the most humane, the most democratic system; it must be able to produce the highest living standards for all its people. Lenin himself said that when that happened, socialism would have gained its historic victory. To achieve it, the Gorbachev reforms are much preferable to the kind of stagnation we have recently seen. I think that competition in the economic, not the military, sphere is in the interests of socialism as a system. It will show its superiority to whatever other system one might suggest. That is one argument, and I have still another.

jkg: Please develop the other point. I'm very much interested.

sm: The question is, how does all this affect revolution and the class struggle? Isn't it in the interests of the working classes and the revolutionary classes in the socialist society to promote political strife in the capitalist world?

I would say that these matters are of no concern for the Soviet Union or for the other socialist countries. The class relationships within the capitalist countries should only be the concern of those countries and of their peoples. The attitude against which I am arguing reflects a very narrow view of the interests of the working classes or of the other revolutionary classes. For myself, I sincerely believe that the first interest of any class in modern society is in maintaining and preserving peace.

JKG: And avoiding nuclear devastation.

SM: And avoiding nuclear devastation. Whatever can be done to prevent that will be in the greatest interest of any social class now in existence.

JKG: I find that a very impressive statement, and again I find myself in agreement. You are obviously moving away from the concept of revolution. Is that general in the Soviet Union?

SM: I think you didn't understand me correctly. We aren't moving away from the concept of revolution. We are saying that peaceful conditions promote the kind of social development that may lead to revolutionary changes in the capitalist countries and perhaps even help accelerate those processes. We don't need to have a period of stagnation, an increase of mass poverty, an increase of strife and generally bad economic and social conditions to promote serious, far-reaching reforms of a socialist nature in the capitalist world.

JKG: I understand. But let me ask another question here. Aren't you a bit out of date in your reference to social classes? In the United States and also in Western Europe the notion of a working class, of a permanent working class, is surely somewhat obsolete. The second generation of workers in manual employments goes on into professional work, into government, into scientific and cultural activities or into management. In the United States their place has been taken in the recent past by new recruits from the rural South; now replacements come in from Mexico and the West Indies. In Europe there is the same kind of turnover. Workers come from other countries. West Germany, for example, doesn't rely solely on German workers but, in very large measure, on Turks, Italians and Yugoslavs. I remember once some years ago the head of the Ford Motor Company in Cologne expressing shock that I would think they used Germans to make automobiles. So I ask you, isn't the notion of social classes in great managerial capitalism now so amorphous as to be obsolete?

sm: I don't think so. By the working class, we mean the vast number of people who live on their wages or salaries rather than on income from property. You are saying that this class isn't permanent, that the workers are mainly immigrants from other countries?

jkg: The working class is in a process of constant transformation.

sm: That's true, the class of people who are hired labor *is* in a process of constant transformation. Its structure is changing in that there is more immigrant labor coming into the developed countries. And it's also true that at one time the hard core of what used to be called the proletariat consisted predominantly of workers employed in the basic industries, and this is less and less so today.

However, the situation itself doesn't basically change; the vast majority of people within the capitalist countries are still people who are living by selling their labor to corporations or private enterprises.

jkg: The point I am making is that this is a very diffuse structure. At any given time, most of its members are in the process of moving themselves or their children into other occupations. They are then replaced by people from rural areas or from the less developed countries.

sm: I understand what you're saying, but I don't think that the sons and daughters of the majority of the people of the first generation move to a very different social position than that of their parents. We will have to check the statistics on that and see whether it's true.

JKG: You seem a bit old-fashioned to me. You are trying to preserve the class struggle.

SM: No, I'm not. And I think you are overdoing the Turkish and Yugoslav examples in West Germany. West Germany has, in fact, cut down on immigrant labor in the recent years of economic stagnation; the basic labor force in West Germany is now German.

JKG: On the contrary, its basic industrial labor force today includes an enormous number of Turks, Italians and Yugoslavs. With your cooperation I am going to arrange to have Marx come back on a visit to the German Federal Republic and see that the industrial reserve army of capitalist West Germany is now partly from communist Yugoslavia. I think he would be impressed by that, don't you?

SM: Perhaps, but what I am saying is that whatever the industrial reserve army, the majority of those presently working in West Germany are now German. The Germans are basically trying to preserve the German character of their labor force.

JKG: I guess we disagree on that, and we will have to look at the figures.

SM: Perhaps when West Germany emerges from its current long period of stagnation, the situation will change. Your analysis was certainly true once, and it may be true again in the future.

JKG: I will concede to you the point that there is probably less reliance on foreign labor now than there was fifteen or twenty years ago.

But there is one other question about the economic relations between our two countries that I would like to raise. It concerns the unwisdom of using trade or the restriction of trade as an instrument of political action. I have reference to the wheat embargo initiated by President Carter and wisely, I think, repealed by President Reagan. And to the now-abandoned effort to persuade our European allies to prohibit equipment from going to that famous pipeline. And to the Jackson-Vanik bill, which denies the Soviet Union a most-favored-nation status in trade because of certain misbehavior on human rights.

I would like to express my own dissatisfaction with such a policy, and I doubt that I will run into very serious disagreement from you. I make the point because you haven't been reluctant to criticize past Soviet policy, so I can't be reluctant to criticize past American policy on these matters. You force me to a very high standard of behavior.

sm: I agree, and I'm glad you have been self-critical. The Soviet Union has never used its trade as a weapon against the United States or, for that matter, against any other country that I can remember. So I would readily agree that neither one of our countries should do so now or in the future.

12

The Superpower Syndrome

SM: I have heard you refer in our previous conversations and also in some of your articles to what you call the superpower syndrome or the superpower mystique. Please tell me what that is.

JKG: There is a common tendency in social comment for nomenclature to lag behind reality, and that is the case with our reference to the so-called superpowers. In fact, in power and influence both the Soviet Union and the United States have been in a process of retreat for the last twenty-five years.

SM: What do you mean by that?

JKG: In your case there has been the great break with China, perhaps the most important single development in foreign affairs in the last quarter century.

SM: That happened a long time ago. But on your side, isn't it true that the peak of American influence in the world, at least economically, was reached fairly soon after the Second World War?

JKG: Let me discuss the position of the United States shortly; first, let me continue with the Soviet Union. You have also seen your influence decline in Egypt and Algeria, in the Far East and Indonesia. And I think there is some doubt as to whether the Soviet presence in Eastern Europe is as great as it was twenty-five years ago.

sm: Obviously you're obsessed with the notion of Soviet power around the world.

jkg: No, I'm prepared to make similar concessions about the United States in just a moment, if you will allow me, but not before I mention one final thing. Although I know only what I read in the newspapers, I gather that you haven't been greeted with overwhelming enthusiasm in Afghanistan.

sm: Why don't you take up the question of Vietnam and the decrease in influence of American imperialism around the world?

jkg: I am by no means reluctant. A quarter of a century ago, we still had Secretary of State John Foster Dulles's web of bilateral treaties, most of which have since disappeared. We had CENTO, of which we were a sponsor in the Middle East, where Iran was our closest ally. And we had SEATO, the treaty in Southeast Asia. Of these we hear no more. We had a solid influence in NATO, which has now weakened somewhat as far as Greece and some other countries are concerned. We had much greater support in Central and South America than we do today. And, meeting your point in my generous way, we encountered disaster in Indochina, particularly in Vietnam.

So what is the picture in the late 1980s? We see both of our countries in a process of retreat, while at the same time the word "superpower" is still being used to describe us. It doesn't reflect the modern reality.

sm: But isn't it true that there continues to be a practical basis for what you call the superpower syndrome? Isn't it true, for that matter, that our countries are still the two largest military powers in the world, the two largest nuclear powers in the world? We are both capable of delivering our nuclear weapons to any spot on the globe, and our nuclear strike capability is much larger than that of France, Great Britain or China, the other nuclear nations. Isn't that what's usually referred to as being a superpower, at least in the military area?

JKG: I wouldn't entirely agree. I would say that the reference to superpower as it developed in the years after World War II denoted a broad influence, indeed some measure of control, over other countries. Powers that were superior to other powers. However, I will concede your point as regards military superiority, this marvelous aggregation of nuclear weapons that neither the Soviet Union nor the United States can use.

SM: I wouldn't like to oversimplify this issue. The rise in the nuclear capability of our two countries has been one serious, objective reason for the deep conflict between the two systems. Perhaps for the first time in modern history a country has appeared that could destroy the United States; you have become vulnerable to bombardment for the very first time. We are equally vulnerable, but we have been endangered by other aggressive countries in the past, so it isn't the first time we have felt threatened.

Because of all this, there has been a definite possibility, at least for a certain period of time, of military conflict, devastating military conflict, between the two countries. I'm glad to say that it now appears that both the United States and the Soviet Union seem to realize the impossibility of such an outcome, and both seem to be pursuing the common aim of reducing their nuclear capability. The objective basis for the clash I was talking about is, we hope, going to recede further in the future if intermediate and, later on perhaps, strategic nuclear weapons are reduced in number or even eliminated.

JKG: I agree with that. But what you're saying is that the

reference to superpowers even at the military level is becoming passé.

SM: It may become passé in the future; that's what I was trying to say. I think it was very real in the past and is still real at the present time.

JKG: You agree with me reluctantly as to the future, and I am prepared to accept even reluctant agreement.

SM: The other basis for this superpower syndrome, as I've said often before, is that, after the Second World War, the United States and the Soviet Union emerged as the leaders of two social systems and as the most powerful countries within those systems. Look at the United States; it has been in continuous expansion and has established its military presence in practically all parts of the world, excluding the socialist countries. It has expanded its economic presence by capturing export markets and increasing its direct investment in foreign countries. This picture is very different from the position the United States had before World War II. And there were some fundamental reasons for that expansion.

One was its obsession with its own military superiority, not only over the Soviet Union but perhaps over the whole world. And there was its increasing economic influence beyond its borders — what I would call the creation of a transnational empire. The United States was willing to support this economic expansion by increasing its political influence. The phrase "America is the leader of the free world" gained wide usage and is still often referred to. The United States promoted its political influence abroad by making other countries dependent on its military power and, to some extent, on its economic and technological potential. That was one driving force which led to the superpower syndrome, wasn't it? And the overall ideological excuse was to stop, contain and throw back communism, socialism.

JKG: Perhaps that was once true, but it's true no longer.

We have now had years of stability as between the socialist-communist and the capitalist systems. No countries of any importance have moved into the socialist camp in recent times, and none from the socialist camp has moved into the capitalist world. So we no longer talk about a socialist take-over or, in your terms, a capitalist counterrevolution.

sм: It's true that wherever the socialist system, which has also become an international system, meets American expansion and wherever the United States feels there is some spread of the socialist system into an area that it considers to be in its sphere of influence, points of conflict do appear. This is what happened in Nicaragua and in Afghanistan.

One can see why the United States would be concerned about the emergence of a society like Nicaragua's, which is different from the structure of the societies around it. And there is an obvious clash of a civil war nature in Afghanistan, with America taking one of the sides and the Soviet Union the other.

jкg: I have long felt that we have an undue fixation on Nicaragua, and I certainly regret the Soviet intervention in Afghanistan. So, I take it, do many people in the Soviet Union. But those countries are hardly considered important players on the world scene. As I say, it's apparent that neither socialism nor capitalism is spreading worldwide.

sм: Basically, you see a picture of a social status quo on an international basis. Is that what you're saying?

jкg: Absolutely. In consequence, what was once thought to be a feature of the superpower situation — a massive socialist dynamic and a massive capitalist dynamic — no longer exists.

sм: But it may be that in the near future or at some more distant time similar conflicts may arise, so we should be aware of them as a possibility. We should, I think, come back to this subject and see how we should deal with these issues if they do come up.

JKG: I agree. However, I seek any comfort I can find in the world situation, and, leaving Nicaragua and Afghanistan aside, I think the danger that the Soviet Union and socialism and the United States and capitalism will clash in some unhappy corner of the world has diminished.

SM: I hope it has. We perhaps forgot to indicate that there are areas where we may be brought into confrontation not so much because of the clash of the social systems themselves or the presence of a civil war but because of other things. Look at the Middle East, where there is a long-standing conflict between some of the countries of the region, with the danger for us of possible military confrontation — the two former superpowers having to take sides in that volatile situation. That's also a danger.

JKG: I don't minimize it. I would point out, however, that in the Middle East the present active conflict, that between Iraq and Iran, isn't at all between capitalism and socialism. It's between two branches of the Islamic faith.

SM: I wasn't just referring to that confrontation but also to the conflict between Israel and some of its neighbors. However, there again there is no obvious conflict between socialism and capitalism.

What I'm saying is that we may be brought into conflict in any part of the world, even though the original clash is between third parties. I think that's a very important point to have in mind for the future of our relations.

JKG: I agree, and it's something that should be a continuing subject of concern.

SM: Why don't we go into some of the causes of what you call the decline of the superpowers and their influence? What was the first cause?

JKG: The first was a factor that was greatly underestimated on both sides after World War II. That was the enormous desire of the smaller national states to be independent of external control. This had brought or helped to bring colonialism to an end, and once that had happened, the former colonial countries didn't want to accept the imperial influence of either of the superpowers.

SM: The Soviet Union and, to some extent, the United States have shown themselves to be in favor of eliminating the colonial system. We have worked together on this within the United Nations. And we in the Soviet Union have supported the cause of national liberation in principle everywhere.

But I agree with you, the picture of the world has drastically changed in the last three quarters of a century. Around the time of the October Revolution in the Soviet Union, the world consisted of a limited number of colonial empires. Now those empires have become one hundred and fifty or more sovereign states. That's something to consider.

JKG: And those one hundred and fifty states defend their sovereignty against both the Soviet Union and the United States.

SM: And against each other, for that matter.

JKG: Yes, the former colonial world is, unfortunately, where wars still continue.

SM: The other cause of the change you mentioned is, I believe, the competition between countries belonging to the same system.

Isn't it true that Japan, West Germany and some of the other capitalist countries are strong competitors of the United States as far as economic relations and market spheres of influence are concerned? Do you consider Japan a threat in that area?

JKG: It certainly isn't a military threat. The Japanese are far too shrewd to devote needed resources to military purposes. As I've said before, that has been one of the reasons for their economic success. However, the point you make is one with which I completely agree and one I would emphasize.

Here in the United States, when we think of economic competition in the world, when a speech on the subject is needed in the Congress, it is Japan of which we think or speak, not the Soviet Union. The economic threat of Japan has, in very substantial measure, replaced the military threat of the Soviet Union in our political psychology. The rise of Japan has been another factor in the decline of what I call the superpower syndrome.

But let me ask you a question here: Hasn't the same thing been true in the Soviet Union? Don't you think of China from time to time when you consider the position of the Soviet Union as a world power?

SM: We don't have much economic competition between the Soviet Union and China in markets or spheres of capital investment; the conflict between the two countries has been largely on ideological grounds. It has been manifest in different attitudes, different points of view on how to develop within the socialist system. It is and has been rather basically an ideological conflict.

JKG: That is my point. As we now have or are coming to have two capitalist superpowers, the United States and Japan, aren't we, to some degree at least, coming to have two socialist superpowers, the Soviet Union and China?

I'm not putting China in the class with Japan as an economic power, but I take it that China is a good deal on the Soviet mind.

SM: It has been for many years. It's a big country and one of our neighbors, but we don't see any threat from China to the Soviet Union. China has been expanding quite successfully in the economic field in the last few years, and it has been experimenting in new forms of socialist management.

JKG: Again my point: we in the United States now see and talk about an economic threat from Japan, and you in the Soviet Union see and talk about an ideological threat from China.

sm: No, we don't talk much about such an ideological threat. The deep differences on how to pursue socialist goals are now largely in the past. The current differences we have between ourselves and China are more in the diplomatic and foreign policy area. Negotiations between the two countries are on such matters as our common frontier, which, in my mind, isn't a problem of particularly great interest or importance; we are talking about minor pieces of territory. The other two bones of contention between us are differences of opinion as to Cambodia and Afghanistan. These are the three basic areas in which the Chinese state disagrees with us. But they are things that have been peacefully discussed for a number of years; we don't see any threat coming from China.

jkg: And I don't see any threat to the United States from Japan; it's a country we greatly admire. But, surely, your world has been carried a long way from Stalin's time, when China, North Korea and North Vietnam were all part of a common socialist system in Asia.

sm: It's true that we had an alliance with China, but it was concluded very soon after World War II. We assisted China economically on a large scale. In fact, the first impetus toward rapid economic development in that country was given largely by the Soviet Union.

I think what we're really facing now is that a number of developed countries within both our systems helped other countries in recovering from the devastation of the last war, only to see the latter become independent economically and politically. There is, of course, nothing wrong in that. It's rather like a father helping his children come of age, only to be surprised by their independent views or independent positions. Didn't the United States put a lot of resources into rehabilitating and reconstructing Japan after the war?

jkg: We came to have a strongly supportive policy toward Japan, but I think it must be said that most of the Japanese recovery was on its own initiative, based on its own efforts.

However, in the first years after World War II, there was surely a bipolar world divided as between the United States and the Soviet Union. Now both capitalism and socialism have multilateral components of great strength, and this is most certainly a further factor in the decline of the superpowers.

SM: We were talking about Japan, but of course we can't forget Western Europe or, for that matter, West Germany. The United States was instrumental, I think, in at least starting the movement toward what you call larger multilateral components by making West Germany one of your competitors in the market. I recall that we in the Soviet Union regarded this postwar policy of assistance to Japan and Germany as one of consciously rehabilitating and reconstructing the two imperialisms, the Japanese and the German, which had been the aggressors in the Second World War. We saw this as a substantial threat to the Soviet Union and perhaps as a design on the part of the United States to strengthen the two big enemies of our country, one on its western border and the other on the east. Here I am coming to another point. It is that the perceptions we have of each other are formed, at least in part, not on an objective but on a subjective basis. Don't you think that's true?

JKG: Absolutely. And I would point out that we saw the Soviet support of China in exactly the same terms as you saw our support of Germany and Japan. For a long while the standard American reference was to a Sino-Soviet bloc — even giving China first place in the reference.

But let me go on to another matter. Although we accept that the circumstances of the superpowers have changed, don't we still have a commitment deep in our cultures to the superpower ideology? I think we do here in the United States. Do you in the Soviet Union?

SM: I think we do, that's true, and it will remain true for a while in the future; we will have to take account of it.

In our discussions we have been considering the current economic situation in the two systems. Obviously we have a difference of views. One of us supports the capitalist way, the other supports the socialist. Now, if I should ask you which system you prefer, your answer would be obvious, and my answer, should you ask me, would also be obvious, but our answers would be different. What that means is that we each still believe, if not in the military, at least in the social and economic superiority of our own system. You believe in your current superiority and we more in our potential superiority. From these beliefs arises an ideological source of conflict that will remain with us for many years.

JKG: I think that's true, but I would add something else. It goes back to the subject we have discussed a good deal — bureaucracy.

When great organizations in your country or in the United States become committed to a mode of thought — and one aspect of that mode of thought in past times has been the notion of the existence of the superpowers and superpower expansion — they don't change. You personally can change your mind, perhaps with some difficulty, and I can change my mind, though with very great difficulty, but it's virtually impossible for a bureaucratic organization to change its mind. So we are still committed bureaucratically as well as culturally to the superpower idea. This is true even after its time has passed, even after we have experienced a great contraction of power on both sides.

SM: Actually, I see large parts of both our societies that don't associate themselves with the bureaucracies and bureaucratic modes of thinking. They aren't part of the bureaucracy; they think along the lines I've indicated before.

They have different views on the future of society. And they are willing to change their minds if they feel they are wrong or that the objective situation has changed.

I believe that we should try to approach the future of capitalism and socialism with a clear mind. May I ask a question? What will the world look like in a hundred years? Will it be all capitalist; will it be all socialist? Will it be a kind of a mixture of both, as it is now, with the two systems coexisting? Will it be one society that has coalesced as a result of the movement of the systems toward each other or will it be two societies that have become even more different from each other? Will it be a different kind of society that we can't even now perceive — the result of the famous Hegelian concept of thesis (capitalism), antithesis (socialism) and synthesis (some kind of a future society, which we may call futurism or something else)? It's something we can only guess at, but what would you say about it?

JKG: Despite my best efforts and determinedly clean living, I don't expect to be around a hundred years from now. Accordingly, I can answer with great confidence, knowing that nobody will be able to come up to me and say with delight that I was wrong.

I would guess that we would have a mixture. There will be a movement to the market in what is now the socialist world along the lines we have previously discussed. There will be a commitment in the capitalist world to greater social concern. And a hundred years from now there will be countries that are still emerging into this more mature combination of socialism and capitalism. Do I make that clear?

SM: Yes, I think you've made yourself clear. I won't be around either in a hundred years to be held responsible for the kind of guesses we're making now, but I generally agree with you that the future will be a mixture of the existing forms, with perhaps some new forms putting in an appearance. I believe that whatever happens then, whichever way society develops, it's important that we now agree that the two systems in the modern nuclear world have no other choice but to follow the paths they are following at the moment. And they have to take very great care that following those paths doesn't lead to military conflict between them.

JKG: I agree with that, and I would say again that I find satisfaction in the notion of superpower retreat instead of superpower expansion. If the latter had continued, eventual conflict would have been inevitable. And I find equal satisfaction in the way in which the Soviet Union is reexamining and modifying its system. Finally, as a long-time socially concerned American liberal, I have great hope that, in the years ahead, we in the United States will resume our search for a socially more just society.

SM: We have talked about the Gorbachev revolution in the field of economics, but there is also a revolution in how the Soviet Union perceives the world and the future of international relations. We call this the new mode of thinking. Perhaps it deserves a special chapter.

JKG: Let's come to that next time.

13

The Conditions for Coexistence

JKG: Yesterday you said that there is a new mode of thinking in the Soviet Union. What exactly is it? How does it bear on the problem of coexistence and, indeed, on the problem of existence itself?

SM: The new mode of thinking may be considered an ideological revolution in our country; it's also something that is very closely connected to the revolution in economic policy. In both cases there is a completely new approach to the reality of the day, a new way of looking at our world and how to exist and coexist in this world in view of the increasing interdependence of all nations and the nuclear reality we have talked about before.

JKG: Let me ask you to be more specific. We have politicians in the United States who regularly say that they're in favor of new thinking. Quite frequently the new thinking turns out to be either old thoughts or something they're too shy to reveal. I can't allow a Soviet visitor to lapse into the generalities of our more evasive public figures.

SM: I don't want to go into all the aspects of the new mode

of thinking as we now see it, but I would like to underscore three salient points at this juncture.

The first is that our two countries should pursue their separate paths. We have shown, in our previous chapters, that each of our systems has its own problems, and each sees that there are various ways of tackling them.

JKG: Specifically, we should both recognize that there can be two economic systems on the planet?

SM: Exactly. But also there has to be a recognition that while we are pursuing our individual paths, we should try not to get into each other's way, not increase each other's difficulties by any deliberate action.

This sounds a bit general, but let me give a few examples. It has been thought that whatever one does within one's own country is one's own business, and for a long time, perhaps, that was correct. The concept of national sovereignty means that the government has an absolute right to pursue whatever it wants to pursue within its own borders. However, we now live in a nuclear world and an interconnected one, interconnected not just in nuclear military matters but also in economic affairs. Let us look first at the military field.

Here actions made on one's own territory directly affect the other's territory. As an example, the intermediate or long-range strategic missiles that are deployed on one side are a direct threat to the security of the other side; they are specifically aimed across the other country's borders. They make it possible to reach and destroy the other country, and when that's possible, it's necessary to stop and think whether one's military actions aren't infringing on the interests of the other side.

JKG: What you're saying is that long-range strategic weapons not only relate to the defense of one's own country but arouse the fears of the other country. That's an obvious point, isn't it?

SM: It *is* an obvious point, but up until now both the

United States and the Soviet Union have been doing exactly that. And they have been not only deploying strategic weapons but sending their navies into the immediate vicinity of each other, maintaining strategic bombing capabilities and so forth. All these actions directly affect the security of the other side. In the future when one country starts to think about its own security, it must think twice and then, before acting, take into account the security of the other.

Let me return to a point I have made previously. Sometimes when one country tries to maximize its short-term interests, it ends up acting in such a way as to undermine its interests in the longer term. In the late sixties and, as I recall, the early seventies, President Nixon decided to deploy the MIRVs [Multiple Independently-Targeted Reentry Vehicles]; he thought by doing so, he would have an advantage over the Soviet Union. However, it took us only a few years to catch up, and what happened was that American security was undermined in exactly the way President Nixon was trying to undermine Soviet security.

JKG: This is your example of the short-run advantage being defeated by the long-run result?

SM: Exactly. That's my first point as to the new mode of thinking. Walk your separate paths, and don't try to antagonize the other side by your actions. Put major emphasis on your long-term interests rather than on your short-term gain. Take into account the interests of the other side since your interests and theirs are interconnected.

JKG: I fully agree. Let's proceed to the second requirement for coexistence.

SM: The second point is to understand that, most probably, we will still be drawn into direct and indirect confrontation. Conflicts will develop in the world. But when they do, it's important to act very differently from the way we've acted in the past. We must stop and think. We mustn't react immediately in an all-out fashion. That could be very dangerous and lead to an escalation of military conflict between our two countries.

This reminds me of an old rule that was introduced by a king in medieval France, where the feudal lords used to fight each other fairly often and wars devastated the countryside. He introduced the so-called Rule of Forty Days of the King, which required that no feudal lord could start a war against another without first thinking about it for forty days. In that way, France was saved from quite a lot of warfare.

JKG: I hadn't previously thought of the need for getting back to feudal times, but I'm prepared to accept the plan. This is the first occasion, however, when somebody from the Soviet Union has come out strongly for feudalism.

SM: Actually, something like the Forty Days exists within the United Nations Charter. The whole procedure in the Security Council is really based on that principle.

JKG: Don't take me too seriously.

SM: The way to act when direct or indirect conflict develops is to consult each other and find a constructive and peaceful solution to the situation, no matter how dangerous it may look at first glance.

JKG: I think that's a very good thought. What's the next thing on your agenda? I will come to my own ideas later.

SM: My third point is that although the two systems are in confrontation and may be in conflict, there are many ways in which we can and must cooperate. The technique of cooperation can be developed more and more so that, as time goes by, we learn to think of each other as partners in progress toward a better world rather than as competitors or enemies.

JKG: This should be especially true in economic matters?

SM: Yes, in such things as developing new energy sources and tackling the problems of underdevelopment and some of the medical issues like cancer, AIDS and narcotic addiction. There are various fields in which we can cooperate.

JKG: I certainly accept that. I have spent a good deal of time in India, and I know we always have a number of Americans who worry constantly about the Soviet influence in that country. I suppose there are an equal number of Soviet citizens who worry about the American influence. You're saying that we should, instead, join together in common support for Indian economic development. And, I suppose I might add, concentrate on providing economic rather than military assistance. Is that right?

SM: I think that's one good example. But I don't want to sound too idealistic.

JKG: Let's not be afraid of being idealistic. Getting rid of ✓ that fear is one of the first things on my list of how we can better and more surely coexist. When somebody tells you you mustn't be idealistic, you can always be sure that he or she is pretty well committed to no change, no improvement in the world.

SM: But I *am* committed to change and improvement in the world. The reason I say let's not be too idealistic is that I think the only chance the principles I have just stated have to be implemented is if the present dangers to coexistence are taken into account and counteracted. They are real, they exist all around us, and we should see them in their correct perspective.

JKG: You say that there are dangers in this whole situation that we must act to counter. Give me some specific examples.

SM: Let's start with perhaps the least dangerous thing in my view, and that is phraseology.

JKG: What we say about each other?

SM: Yes, exactly. Once in a while we hear remarks from the other side that we take to be insulting or aggressive.

You remember when Mr. Khrushchev came to the United States and one of his statements was translated as, "We will bury you." This was taken by many Americans to mean that the Soviet Union was out to destroy the United States and kill and bury Americans.

JKG: I certainly remember that. It was a great encouragement to our cold war attitudes.

SM: I must say that I'm pretty sure Mr. Khrushchev didn't mean it that way, but the unfortunate expression he used led the American public to believe that that was what, in fact, he had on his mind.

There is another famous example in "the Evil Empire," a phrase used by President Reagan a few years ago. We know that he said it in the context of a kind of theological speech, and it was understood in the Soviet Union to mean that ours was an empire that belonged to the Devil or was created by the Devil, and Reagan was something like the . . .

JKG: The destroying avenger, the righteous, opposing God.

SM: Exactly, exactly; the phrase had aggressive overtones that were taken quite seriously by the Soviet Union.

JKG: Again I tend to agree. Maybe I would add that we should learn to ignore rhetoric of this kind in this age of *glasnost*. In the United States we are always going to have people, including politicians, who make disagreeable and provocative comments.

SM: But apart from rhetoric and phraseology, there are a lot of other, more important dangers. One of them is the continuing armaments race. We are still increasing our armaments; the nuclear arsenal is still growing; the nuclear tests are still proceeding — all in spite of the agreement on intermediate nuclear weapons. The arsenals of conventional weapons have also not been dismantled, there are a lot of conventional forces being maintained, and a great number of chemical weapons on both sides that probably aren't going to be used are still being produced. And the Star Wars program is being developed. All this is a menace to the world. I remember before World War I, the Balkans were described as sitting on a barrel of gunpowder. Now it's not just the Balkans, it's the whole world, all of civilization, that's sitting on an arsenal of nuclear arms that can destroy civilization at any point by sheer error.

JKG: War by mistake.

SM: I think that's a very important point. We have to curb the armaments race; it's one of the first exigencies of our program.

JKG: Let me press a point there too. I think we agreed that we would leave the inner theology of arms control to other discussants, but I have two thoughts, one of which I may have mentioned before.

I'm disturbed by the number of people nowadays who ∨ seem to think that conventional armies are benign. I'm old enough to remember two world wars, both of them fought, in the main, with conventional forces. I have the feeling that the people who got killed in those wars are just as dead as if they had been killed with nuclear weapons.

I don't suppose any single confrontation in this century was more disastrous than the first day of the Battle of the Somme in World War I, when nearly twenty thousand British soldiers were killed in successive waves going against the entrenched machine guns. Today we see masses of teenagers being killed in a war that is being fought with conventional weapons between Iran and Iraq. I would like to see more discussion of the dangers and the evil effects of conventional warfare.

SM: The Soviet Union lost twenty million people in World War II, and that was a conventional war.

JKG: A very good point.

My other thought is that I am puzzled as to why the Soviet Union makes such an issue of Star Wars — what Washington calls the Strategic Defense Initiative. There is a widespread impression in the United States that it won't work; in fact, that's the best scientific opinion being expressed in our country. And of course it will cost us a great deal of money. Why is the Soviet Union pressing an issue about which we should be more worried ourselves? Would you explain it?

SM: I think the logic here is slightly different from your view of the matter. If we were sure that your program would be a flop, a complete disaster, we wouldn't worry. However, it's bound to produce a new generation of weapons, and while some of those weapons may not be all that effective in countering missiles shot at the United States from the other side, they could, in fact, be used from outer space as a menace to us. I'm thinking specifically about laser and kinetic weapons deployed in space and aimed at Soviet territory. That's one point, and there is special concern in our country about it.

Also, while you may not be particularly worried about the waste of your resources — you're used to wasting resources since they have always been so plentiful — your space program will feed the appetites of those in the Soviet Union who claim that we must now have our own Star Wars. Such a program in our case would take a lot of resources away from civilian uses, which we now consider a major priority in our society. These are the two basic points I would like to make.

But maybe one final thing. I feel that the problem isn't just your propensity for wasting resources. I think your weapons manufacturers have a deep vested interest in a totally assured market for the next couple of decades; they see Star Wars as a tremendous bonanza and a very profitable area of business for years to come.

JKG: You don't think they're just generous people who want to help your hard-liners?

SM: I don't know; I don't think so. I think it's profits they have in mind.

JKG: I'm willing to accept your help in bringing Star Wars to an end, but now let me suggest what I see as some of the dangers to coexistence that need to be overcome.

I harbor the impression, indeed the belief, that we have vested interests in tension and conflict on both sides of the superpower relationship, if I may still use that term. Some of those interests we have already mentioned.

sм: You mean that of the military-industrial complex?

jкg: The military-industrial complex in the United States does have such a vested interest, and it has been evident in our conversation that this is a bilateral situation, that that vested interest exists on both sides. There is also in our country, and I would suppose in the Soviet Union as well, what we might call a vested intellectual interest in disagreement, tension and conflict.

sм: What does that mean?

jкg: We have people who have devoted their lives to warning of the dangers of communism and world communism, and I venture to think you have people on your side — journalists, academic people, others — who have devoted their careers to warning of the dangers of capitalist imperialism.

sм: Don't those people feed on deep suspicions within our populations, which have been caused by a lot of loose talk in the mass media?

jкg: And even in the scholarly journals — absolutely. But having those beliefs and having held them for a lifetime, they don't want to change.

I know some academic figures in the United States, quite a few, who, if hostility between our two countries were to diminish, would then have to deny what they have always written and taught. I feel somewhat sorry for them, although I can contain my grief. I can understand how it's necessary for them to believe that continued tension proves they have always been right.

sм: Perhaps they're too old to change. Maybe the younger ones will pursue a more constructive path.

JKG: I hope that will be the case, and age, of course, eventually has its own, somewhat inconvenient corrective of error.

Next I would cite another danger that I don't think can be mentioned often enough. We have used in these discussions the word "bureaucracy" to the point that it is surely developing a certain tedium, but one must stress again that organizations generally persist in one mode of thought and have great difficulty changing to another. The person within an organization who suggests something different is looked upon as an eccentric.

SM: Could you perhaps give some examples?

JKG: I have in mind the commitment by the Pentagon and in perhaps lesser measure by the State Department to the idea of enduring hostility with the Soviet Union. I venture to think that a similar situation may not be entirely foreign to your experience.

SM: Yes, there are some common professional characteristics of people working in the field of defense that make them somewhat one-sided in their approach to wider problems. They take the military side seriously. They don't sometimes perceive the broader implications of the arms issues they are supporting.

JKG: I'm glad we're able to find similarities in our systems once again.

SM: You seem to be a bit fatalistic. Since in both our systems the various bureaucracies wield a large amount of power, it looks as if they represent a real danger to coexistence. How can this danger be overcome?

JKG: I'm not wholly pessimistic. I'm concerned but not pessimistic. The way it's overcome in our society is by the force of political will — in this case, the political will to reach an accommodation with the Soviet Union. For the American people as a whole the idea of nuclear euthanasia and death is not politically very popular. Accordingly, we already have in the making a strong political movement toward accommodation. As I've said before, we will have a presidential election in 1988, and most of the relevant candidates will be talking about the need for arms control and for ensuring against nuclear destruction.

sm: I believe a good example of political will on our side is Mr. Gorbachev, who, since becoming General Secretary, has been very effective in turning the tide in the general conception of foreign policy in our country and in curbing some of what you referred to as bureaucratic inertia in the perception of international issues. It's important that he's getting the overwhelming support of our people on that.

jkg: Another thing I would like to urge as one of the escapes from danger is a greater emphasis on long-term interests. We talked in an earlier conversation about what the world would be like a hundred years from now. I venture to think that if there has been no nuclear confrontation by then, people will look back on the present tension between the Soviet Union and the United States as a rather minor matter. If, however, there *has* been a nuclear war, those who survive, if any, will look back upon that war as a truly major event. So I would urge that we see our present differences, great or small, in the long perspective of history. They are bound to seem very slight as compared with a nuclear disaster. Do you agree?

sm: Yes, I generally agree. And I believe there is a great example of the exercise of political will in the history of your country. President Franklin Roosevelt was one of your politicians who had the political will to curb the power of the bureaucracies. I remember that before going to Yalta, he got considerable advice from most of the people around him. They said he would have to take a very firm, if not rigid, position vis-à-vis the Soviet Union, which was at that time emerging in the eyes of many as a military danger to the United States. However, he disregarded that advice, and he went to Yalta with Stalin and Churchill, and together they laid the foundation of a peaceful structure for the coming decades — what eventually became the United Nations.

You know, people sometimes say that we haven't had a war in the last forty years because there has been a balance of terror. I don't agree with that. I believe that, basically, we haven't had a real confrontation because a peaceful structure was created by leaders who had the political will to do so.

JKG: Some revisionists have given the name Yalta an evil connotation, but I think we need to remember that those wartime meetings were a good example of how we can pursue a larger objective — in that case, dealing with Hitler and National Socialism — and at the same time subordinate the lesser but not insignificant differences that otherwise would divide the participants. Those of us who were alive in those years will remember Teheran and Yalta not as failures but as achievements.

SM: Yes; then came Potsdam. The Potsdam Agreements were signed by President Truman, a man whom the Soviet Union doesn't remember as being especially friendly. However, he did sign those agreements, and that was an act of wisdom on his part.

JKG: You must allow me an anecdote here.

SM: Go ahead.

JKG: I was in Europe with the United States Strategic Bombing Survey at that time. One of my colleagues was George Ball, whom you have met. He called me up one morning and said, "Do you realize that the great men of Europe are meeting next week to settle the future of the world?" I replied, "Of course. I read *Stars and Stripes*."[1] He said, "I think we should attend," to which I replied, "But

---

1. The army newspaper.

we haven't been invited." He said, "If we allow hurt feelings to stand in the way of our going, we will just compound their error in not inviting us." Since we had an airplane at our disposal, we flew to Berlin, along with Paul Nitze, the arms negotiator of much recent mention, and we all went out to the American compound. A friend of mine there named Isador Lubin asked me to join him on the Reparations Commission. Ball and Nitze became similarly involved. Our stay was brief, but that is how in those days one managed to attend summit conferences.

sm: I wasn't fortunate enough to go to the Potsdam meetings. However, as a young man, a student, soon after the war, I was a member of the staff on the Soviet delegation in Moscow at one of the meetings of what was called the Council of Foreign Ministers of the Great Powers. These were the Soviet Union, the United States, Great Britain and France. It was quite an experience seeing how the ministers of those countries worked together. That was the very beginning of the cold war, but they still got together and tried to solve the common issues.

jkg: Our representative was Secretary of State George Marshall?

sm: No, it was Secretary Byrnes. James Byrnes for the United States, Georges Bidault for France, Ernest Bevin for Great Britain and Vyacheslav Molotov for our country.

I believe that our alliance during the war and the solution of common issues when the war was over are a perfect example of how two opposing systems can cooperate. The social structures of Germany and Japan were, in fact, closer to that of the United States, for all were capitalist societies, but you, as a capitalist society, cooperated with the socialist society to eliminate fascism. That was a perfect example of how we can work together.

jkg: All of my generation remember that June day in 1941, when word came that the Soviet Union was in the war on our side as a result of Hitler's invasion of Russia. I was living that summer in northern Virginia and commuting to Washington, and I heard the news on the radio. For the first time I felt there might be hope; until then the war prospect had looked extremely grim, indeed.

Let me add just one point here. The Soviet Union and the United States joined together to deal with the menace of Adolf Hitler, but even that menace could hardly compare with the threat of nuclear war. Let us, on occasion, reflect on that.

sm: In modern times John Kennedy was perceived in our country as the kind of American President who was ready to bring the two countries into a state of acute confrontation. So he was at the time of the Cuban missile crisis. He then tried to resolve the crisis in a way that was in the interests of both sides and proceeded to conclude one of the greatest agreements of our time, the agreement to ban nuclear tests.

jkg: The Limited Test Ban Treaty.

sm: It's limited, but for all practical purposes, it cleaned the atmosphere of the planet from nuclear contamination. That was a great, great achievement.

jkg: Kennedy told me, as he told many others, that he never wanted to wake up a single morning without thinking what could be done that day to lessen the danger of nuclear war.

sm: Whatever you may think of President Nixon, he and General Secretary Brezhnev will go into history as the architects of détente in the early 1970s, and this, too, was a really positive development.

jkg: I have never been an ardent supporter of President Nixon's, but I give him credit for that. And to him and Henry Kissinger I give great credit for opening up relations with China. That was something that should have been done earlier by my Democratic colleagues.

But to go on. There is another danger of which we must

be aware. It's one we've talked about before. We mustn't allow ourselves to get involved on different sides of the conflicts between other countries.

One of the sad features of our time is that while nobody has been killed in a war between the Soviet Union and the United States, there have been very many regional conflicts between and within smaller countries in which a great number of people have been killed. Let us both be aware of the danger that can come from getting involved on the opposite sides of those conflicts — in the Middle East, Asia or wherever.

I cite as examples Vietnam and Indochina in the past and, of course, Afghanistan now. I would like to see a general rule, a general understanding, that we both are going to move back from the internal conflicts of other countries. Would you agree with that?

SM: I not only agree with it, I think much more is needed. We must act in a very positive and constructive way in trying to bring an end to military hostilities between and within other countries. We mustn't regard them as something distant and not concerning ourselves.

Let me cite the example of the war between India and Pakistan in the mid-1960s. You may recall that the Soviet Union took the initiative in bringing the two countries together and, in fact, brought them to a peaceful solution. Our Premier, Mr. Kosygin, went to Tashkent together with the Prime Minister of India and the representatives of Pakistan. There an agreement was quickly reached that led to the termination of military hostilities between the two countries.

But closer to the present day, we should do more to settle the conflict in the Middle East, for it's really getting out of hand. I know for a while the United States took the position that they could unilaterally resolve the issues dividing Israel and its neighbors, although the Soviet Union wanted very much to cooperate in that effort. There was a reluctance on the part of the United States to cooperate with us because evidently you believed that this would increase the influence of the Soviet Union in the region. I think that that reluctance remains, and it's one example of where we see each other in terms of confrontation. That view precludes both of us from helping terminate a conflict that has really become a sore on the body of that part of civilization.

JKG: In the United States we intend to continue close relations with Israel; much past history is involved and a great emotional commitment. However, at a minimum, we mustn't think of the Middle East as an area of conflict between capitalism and communism. I venture the thought that nothing could be quite as troublesome for communism as, say, a communist Iran.

SM: Since we're talking about regional issues, let me bring up a question that I've had on my mind since one of our previous discussions. You made a comment to the effect that you hoped we would see a kind of international status quo as far as the two systems are concerned, meaning the expansion of the two systems.

Now, being quite realistic, I wouldn't preclude the possibility that changes in the international balance between the nations may occur. Suppose, for example, that in the not too distant future, in some country somewhere in the world — Latin America, Africa or Asia, it's not important where — a government comes to power of the type of Salvador Allende's in Chile in the 1970s. How would the United States approach that kind of a situation? Would you handle it the same way you did Mr. Allende or, say, Grenada later on? What would be your attitude? If it were the same as in Grenada and Chile, it would create additional friction between our countries, which to my mind would be unfortunate.

JKG: I wrote to the *New York Times* immediately after the Grenada invasion regretting it. I similarly regret the action we took against Allende, particularly because I believe that if a government comes to power by democratic process, we must accept it. Allende may not have been the best possible choice for Chile, but that wasn't for us to decide. I would expect a similar kind of restraint on the part of the Soviet Union.

SM: There are also cases where governments come to power not exactly by what you call democratic or parliamentary means but by way of revolution, and this leads to a civil war between two factions, one of which may be socialist or communist and the other procapitalist. That kind of thing could lead to increasing friction between the two systems.

JKG: I'm in favor of our both keeping out; in fact, I strongly so urge. But I would stress again something we talked about earlier. In the Third World I don't consider socialism or communism a viable choice in the elementary stages of economic development. Again I cite Marx: socialism and communism are not possible until after there has been capitalism.

In the United States we once wasted a great deal of time worrying about whether the Belgian Congo, now Zaire, might become communist; I believe that that was never a possibility.

SM: As a scholar and political figure, you aren't very much scared by the shadow of communism, I know, but . . .

JKG: I'm not scared by the shadow of communism where there hasn't been capitalism.

SM: I mean by the general shadow of communism. There are many people in the United States who still view communists as their enemy. Once when I was working at the United Nations in the seventies, I got in a taxi at Kennedy Airport to be driven home. The taxi driver, who had apparently been watching the television news, said, "Look here, the Commies are in Angola now; tomorrow they will be in Brooklyn." That kind of psychology.

JKG: Some people gain all their wisdom from New York cab drivers. I don't want you to be one of them.

SM: What I am saying is that he got his wisdom from the mass media in the United States, and the mass media get their wisdom from the vested interests you were talking about earlier.

JKG: Let me suggest that we go on to another danger.

SM: In the case of Grenada, one of the reasons given for intervention was that the United States armed forces were defending American property and American citizens in that country. Now, there is a lot of American property and investment abroad. And there are a lot of American citizens in other countries. I would think that in any regional conflict that broke out, there would be a great danger of direct American military intervention based on what I would call a kind of *pax Americana* psychology. I would urge that you should take a much saner view of the dangers to America that arise in areas subject to local conflict.

JKG: As a practical matter, I wouldn't exclude the need to rescue American citizens who are caught up in some disastrous situation. I would hope that our doing so wouldn't be taken as an exercise in American imperialism.

SM: Arthur Schlesinger refers to "the superpower fallacy" rather than to American imperialism, and I think perhaps he has a good point.

JKG: We will have to count him a supporter of our views on the superpower syndrome.

But let me raise another matter, one we have perhaps postponed too long. If we're going to minimize conflict between our two countries, we must recognize that we both have internal policies that can still be very damaging to our relations. I have in mind human rights. Could I say a word about that?

SM: Sure, go ahead.

JKG: It's something on which we must take a sane view. We have problems of human rights in the United States, particularly as regards our minorities and the lives they live in the big cities. We also have a certain number of people who flog the Soviet Union for shortcomings in the area of civil rights, not because they're particularly concerned about human rights but because it's a handy weapon. I've always been distressed by how many people attack the Soviet Union for such flaws and are quite tolerant of much worse human rights abuse in, say, South Africa. Nonetheless, since the days of Stalin, there has been real concern by men and women of good and civilized views about the human rights problem in the Soviet Union. This is an example of an internal policy with external effect. Can you give me some hope on that?

SM: Let me put it this way. There is also concern in the Soviet Union about human rights in the capitalist countries, including the United States, especially on economic matters, and I would like to say here that it's a two-sided, not a one-sided, issue.

JKG: I concede that point. To be without money, without any means of support, is a grave limitation on an individual's freedom; I don't deny it. But I want to get back to the Soviet Union.

SM: What I had particularly in mind is that the United States has, I believe, failed to ratify one of the covenants of the United Nations which calls for economic and social rights for people everywhere.

But let's go back to the Soviet Union. Of course one should realize that our country has come a long way since the days of what was called the Red Terror — the revolutionary ter-

ror in the civil war — and the cult of personality under Stalin. Many illegal happenings in those days are long past, but
we still don't have a perfect judicial system. This doesn't only
pertain to what are called dissidents or minority groups but
to other inadequacies that are being widely discussed in the
Soviet press at this moment as a result of the *glasnost* policy.

Now let me say that in January of this year (1987) Mr.
Gorbachev made a special point of accenting the development of democracy within our system. He later stressed that
democracy and the economic reforms are the main interconnected objectives of the current revolution. Democracy
will be one of the major tools for fighting the negative aspects
that have come with bureaucracy, of which the cult of personality was perhaps one. So we are moving in the right
direction.

You may know that some things, like choosing between
two candidates instead of voting for just one, are being introduced in elections in the Soviet Union. There is much
more freedom of expression in the press nowadays. And
there are other areas in which the human rights situation is
being corrected. So I have great hopes. I don't know whether
your people have as much hope as to what is happening in
our country, but I have great hope for progress in the area
of human rights there.

JKG: When I was in the Soviet Union last winter, I was
struck with how much more freedom of discussion there
was than there had been on my earlier visits, how much
more aggressive was the criticism of the system that one
encountered. And I might also add that I noticed how frequently black humor, as we call it, was brought to bear on
the system.

But let me ask one other question, which has been very
much on my mind over the years. How do you see the
prospect for the emigration of people who want to move

out of the U.S.S.R., and especially the people who want to
go to Israel?

SM: I think that that matter is being cleared up right now.
The rules for emigration have been made more liberal, and
I feel there is progress in that field.

You should realize that the issue of emigration touches a
very delicate point in the consciousness of our people. In
the United States when they talk about emigration from the
Soviet Union, they usually point to specific ethnic groups
within the country.

JKG: I just did, as a matter of fact.

SM: But you must realize that all citizens should, in principle, be equal and that every one of them, not just two or
three ethnic groups, should have the right to emigrate. We
have a population of two hundred and eighty million, and
the number of people who actively want to emigrate is way
below half a million. It's a delicate and not very simple question as far as the psychology of the whole population is
concerned, but I think there is progress there.

JKG: Again, if I may, a personal anecdote. I have always
been in favor of free movement across national frontiers. I
was brought up in Canada, where we traveled back and forth
to the United States with a maximum of disdain for any legal
prohibitions. In my youth it was customary to seek employment in Detroit in the fall and winter and not wholly unusual
to vote in the Canadian elections in spring or summer and
then vote in the American elections in November. I have
never thought that a uniquely wicked situation.

SM: No, not at all. And there is a lot more movement
across the Soviet borders now than there was in the past.
I'm talking here about tourism, about people going to other
countries on the invitation of their friends or relatives who
live abroad. I must say, however, that we have a significant
economic limitation on such travel. Although our balance

of payments deficit is not as large as yours, we do have a problem. You are easily underwriting your deficit by allowing the Japanese to buy up your companies and government securities, but we take the different view that we aren't exactly ready to jeopardize our own country's economic system. So we're striving to move toward a convertible ruble, and we're instituting more lenient rules about the amount of currency a man or woman can exchange when going abroad.

We are in favor of a generally convertible currency. A convertible ruble is one of the official aims of Mr. Gorbachev's economic reforms, and as we progress toward it, there will be more and more freedom of movement of our people across the borders to both socialist and capitalist countries.

JKG: I know that our discussions have contained some novelties, but I'm especially interested in the thought that the Japanese might also take over *your* balance of payments deficit.

SM: When we mention Japan and perhaps Western Europe, one idea comes to my mind as a further danger to coexistence. At the time the détente of the early seventies was developing, there was a lot of concern, particularly in Western Europe, about what was seen as the danger of combining the American transnational corporations with a communist bureaucracy. The rapprochement between the United States and the Soviet Union was thought to be creating a kind of Soviet-American condominium, that is, a scheme for dividing the world between the two large superpowers. That was a factor, I believe, that unduly and unnecessarily influenced our relations in the wrong direction.

JKG: This is important. We must have it understood that we aren't engaged in dividing up the world. I confess that I still think you personally have transnational or multinational corporations too much on your mind. But I think the fear of what might happen as the result of a better association between the Soviet Union and the United States is not now very great. I believe most people in Western Europe would welcome a rapprochement between our two countries. I hope they would.

SM: One way of bringing it about is to encourage more constructive cooperation between us and, in fact, make this cooperation part of a global cooperative effort in which other countries would participate actively and on an equal footing. Perhaps then we would find solutions for all our problems.

14

Terms of Cooperation

JKG: Let us now, as we come toward the end of our conversations, turn to fully affirmative steps. How, as tension diminishes, and we hope it will diminish, can our two countries cooperate? Since we're both economists, I suppose we will have economic matters primarily in mind, but let's not confine ourselves to those.

Am I right that there is hope in the Gorbachev reforms for increased economic association between the socialist and the capitalist worlds?

SM: That is absolutely correct. The Gorbachev reforms provide for two important developments in international economics. One is legislation that makes it possible for enterprises in the Soviet Union to work directly with foreign firms in the area of international trade, whereas previously there was a monopoly by the state Ministry of Foreign Trade.

JKG: The enterprise can now go to the foreign seller rather than to the government ministry?

SM: It goes directly to the foreign seller or the foreign buyer rather than going through the ministry. At least that's what's conceived to be the case for most of the larger en-

terprises. The smaller enterprises will still have to avail themselves of the middlemen. These are the different firms
belonging to the Ministry of Foreign Trade that specialize
in the export or import of a particular group of commodities.

JKG: What is the other development?

SM: The second major point is legislation that makes it
possible for our enterprises to set up joint enterprises with
foreign firms, both outside the Soviet Union and in our own
territory.

We have had joint enterprises in other countries before,
for example, in Britain, Belgium and a number of other
European countries. The one in Belgium is particularly concerned with selling cars of Soviet make in foreign markets.

What we're talking about now is setting up joint enterprises in Soviet territory, and that's a significant new development. It gives the foreign corporations a chance to
participate in the Soviet economy by investing capital in our
industries or, for that matter, in trade or whatever other
area is in need of development.

JKG: You no longer see these joint enterprises as centers
of subversive capitalist activity?

SM: We hope they won't be, but let me say that, by law,
foreign participation will be limited to forty-nine percent of
total capital, and we will leave to ourselves the controlling
share of fifty-one percent. Nonetheless, forty-nine percent
is quite a large part, and it ensures nearly equal participation
for the investors of foreign capital.

JKG: As a practical matter and from long experience in
these matters, I would say that ultimate control is ensured
to the one who assumes the most aggressive leadership in
the operation. The difference between forty-nine and fifty-
one percent ownership is, in most cases, wholly unimportant.
Would you agree?

SM: I believe that the most important thing is who controls

the management of the firm. It's required by law that the general manager be a Soviet citizen. Vast participation by foreigners is, however, also provided for, and that, I believe, will ensure equal control and more or less equal partnership.

The hope is that the creation of such joint enterprises will lead to an expansion of trade between the Soviet Union and the capitalist countries, including the United States and other major partners. Right now our principal capitalist partner is the Federal Republic of Germany. We feel that trade with that country still needs to be expanded, but we also feel that there is a great possibility to increase trade with the United States.

JKG: I hope that will be the case. But let's be specific. What do you have to sell that we can buy in increased quantities? Obviously one of the principal forms of cooperation we can render on economic matters is to buy Soviet products. What do you have in volume to sell?

SM: That's the question an American usually asks, and I must say it's not a simple one to answer. You have to realize that most of the foreign trade of the Soviet Union up until recently has been oriented toward other socialist countries. Their share of our exports was once somewhere around seventy to eighty percent and is still very close to that amount. Now, as you may know, there isn't very strong competition between socialist countries; markets aren't really fought for but are developed as a result of long-term agreements.

Most of our exports to the developed capitalist countries in the last decade have been either fuel, like petroleum or gas, or raw materials. In both cases marketing has been relatively simple. These are products the quality of which is more or less easy to ascertain and the price of which is generally the established world price. All you have to do is deliver your commodity to a known international center for the sale or purchase of that particular commodity.

JKG: I understand all that. But the future surely lies in

manufactured products and particularly, I suppose, in consumer goods.

sm: I guess so. We have been successful in expanding our exports of equipment to less developed countries, that's true, but, except perhaps in a few cases, we haven't been successful in selling manufactured products in the West or in Japan. Weapons sales may be one exception, but they're not something we should be striving to expand. I think weapons sales should be limited by agreement between our two countries, don't you?

jkg: I'm certainly not enthusiastic about increased weapons sales. But I must get you back to capital equipment and also consumer goods. With consumer goods there is this constant problem of accommodating to new styles and designs and creating new products that will serve changing consumer taste and that require salesmanship. We no longer devise a new product or even change a design without, on occasion, spending as much money on advertising, getting it on television, as we do on the production itself. How do you propose to contend with that situation?

sm: We don't have too much experience in doing that kind of job in the world market, but that's exactly where the joint enterprise comes in. We want to learn from the marketing experience of foreign management, and we hope that the participation of foreign management in the joint enterprises will be a substantial factor in solving the marketing problem.

jkg: You envisage that you will produce the goods and the foreign part of the joint management will, initially at least, be responsible for the advertising, the merchandising and the selling of the products?

sm: We hope that all parts of the operation will be handled jointly by the partners in the sense that we would have the foreign management participate in the production of goods as well. In that way, we will take advantage of its

experience in that area. The American, Japanese and Western European countries have had quite a lot of experience
in the management of output. And we would also want to
learn from them the tricky art of salesmanship.

JKG: You see the joint venture as being, at least in part,
an educational enterprise?

SM: It's educational, but it's also, in a very practical sense,
an economic enterprise. We hope that it won't be just export-
or import-oriented but that there will be a large spin-off to
all parts of our economy. It would be a good school for our
management in developing market relationships and making our country more consumer-oriented as we develop in
the economic sphere. I think this would clear up a lot of the
misunderstanding we have with the United States. If, as a
companion development, we both could then reduce our
share of military expenditure, it would be a fine thing and
a very solid basis for economic cooperation.

JKG: I suppose there are some people, including some of
my own countrymen, who would say that even a less planned
economy in the Soviet Union isn't a very hospitable environment for the so-called free enterprise corporation.

A long-time friend of mine, Donald Kendall of Pepsico,
has had no slight success in converting Russians from vodka
to Pepsi-Cola, but I wonder if other firms might find this
kind of thing difficult. What do you have to say about that?

SM: We have heard some queries of this sort, not so much
from corporate officials as from the ideological establishment in the United States. One complaint is that conditions
are much better for corporations in the capitalist world than
they are in the Soviet Union. Why go into a planned economy when there are plenty of possibilities elsewhere?

My answer is that there are some objective difficulties on
both sides, and these shouldn't be underestimated. How does
a large modern capitalist corporation fit into our planned
system? What if the Gosplan starts giving orders to the joint

enterprise, and the foreign management isn't particularly happy about it? And what about the different status of labor as between the joint enterprises and the national enterprises inside the Soviet Union? There are many difficult issues, but I think that all of them can be worked out with the cooperation of both sides. The basic thing is that there is a vast possibility for both of us to expand into new markets.

JKG: And beyond that, it's a bona fide move toward cooperation.

SM: Exactly. A few hundred firms have, in fact, already made it clear that they intend to set up joint enterprises with the Soviet Union. That's a sign that whatever some members of the ideological establishment think or say, the businessman sees a new, very important area to develop.

JKG: We might note in passing that this isn't an entirely new circumstance. One of my most admired friends over the years was Averell Harriman. He went to Russia to set up a joint mining enterprise in the 1920s, didn't he?

SM: His father or someone else in the family had started a joint enterprise that had to do with manganese mines in the republic of Georgia. Mr. Harriman came over in the midtwenties to supervise it, and he found that conditions at that time for what were called concessions weren't particularly satisfactory.

JKG: But he worked on it for a time?

SM: That particular concession was, in fact, terminated after a number of years. But you're correct in saying that in the 1920s under Lenin, foreign concessions were allowed in our country, and they were helpful to our development in many ways.

JKG: I want to come back to another thought about lines of cooperation, one we have touched on before. That is the possibility of an infusion of students from the Soviet Union into our business schools. Unfortunately, I'm not authorized to say how many the Harvard Business School could accommodate, but I do think the idea of a certain number of Russian applicants each year might be entirely agreeable.

SM: We have a number of business schools for various levels of management in the Soviet Union, but I agree that some of the people aspiring to managerial jobs should, in fact, be trained or at least partly trained in the United States. Some of our students have gone to your business schools already, including one or two people who went through Harvard Business School, but they are few in number. I believe it would be very helpful for more students to avail themselves of that possibility.

JKG: We would have to be concerned, as we talk, that they not be snatched up by Goldman, Sachs.

I take it, Dr. Menshikov, that this cooperation is not going to be an easy process. I suppose one favorable feature from our point of view — or at least from the point of view of some American businessmen — is that we needn't fear that we're building up a new competitor, that you're going to be a new Japan. Am I right in thinking that we can take a rather sanguine view of our ability to survive Soviet competition?

SM: I am surprised by you, Professor Galbraith. You have said in a number of our previous discussions that you're an internationalist and you don't see anything wrong with Japanese or West German transnational corporations invading the American market or, in fact, buying up Goldman, Sachs and all the other Wall Street firms.

But, seriously speaking, the danger of the Soviet Union taking over the American economy is very remote, and I wouldn't bother about it at this moment, if I were you.

JKG: Now let us turn to what we in the capitalist countries will get out of this because I would like to think of it as a two-sided operation. We could look forward to an expanded market for our consumer goods if there were an increase in trade with the Soviet Union, couldn't we?

SM: That's a possibility. Once we increase our potential for selling in foreign markets and our ability to earn hard currency in those markets, we will have a much wider capacity to buy whatever consumer or producer goods we need that are available in the United States.

JKG: And we would have a better assured market for our farm products too, wouldn't we?

SM: That may happen, and it may become a little bit more sophisticated. Right now we just buy wheat or corn from you because of the inadequate output of our own agriculture. In the future there could be a more complicated exchange, which would include other products of both American and Soviet agriculture.

JKG: I suppose that another of our specific gains would be in the area in which our economy is now showing its greatest current achievement, and that is in the large service enterprises.

SM: What do you have specifically in mind?

JKG: I am thinking of service and franchise operations. These have extended greatly into Europe, even slightly into Japan and now would have an enormous opportunity in the Soviet Union. I envisage a McDonald's on Red Square just opposite the Kremlin.

SM: We already have fans of McDonald's and other similar enterprises in our country, but let me tell you I'm a little concerned about the direction you're trying to drive us in.

We have had experience in the last few years of being cut off from higher technology sales in the West, and I must say that one of the major benefits the Soviet economy would expect from an expansion of trade would be greater imports and exports of high technology. I feel you are trying to drive us toward the McDonald's syndrome and rather away from the high technology syndrome. Isn't that something that the government of the United States is doing right now with the Toshiba incident?[1]

JKG: I wasn't particularly determined to confine you to McDonald's; I consider your charge unjust. The point you mention is one I've talked about with my scientific and engineering colleagues over these last months and years. I would be in favor of a much more relaxed exchange of technical knowledge with your country and larger sales of technologically sophisticated products.

It's one of the myths of our time that we can keep technological developments to ourselves. There may be something possible in this regard as concerns military weaponry but not much even there. The singular feature of technological development, as I think I've mentioned before, is the lightning speed with which it moves across international frontiers. That it can somehow be kept as a monopoly of one country is one of our greatest fantasies. So I would be fully agreeable to going beyond McDonald's to a wide range of cooperation on technological, scientific and engineering developments.

SM: The Toshiba incident is interesting because it's a case where the Pentagon has been particularly vocal about American national security interests having been endangered by trade between Japan and the Soviet Union.

But let me give you an example where there are obviously no strategic considerations, and still they are put forward. Recently the Soviet Union applied to participate in the Multifiber Arrangement, which is an agreement within GATT [General Agreement on Tariffs and Trade] to control the international trade in textiles. Now, textiles aren't a strategic

1. The strongly adverse reaction on the part of the American government to the sale by the Japanese of advanced technology to the Soviet Union.

commodity — they have absolutely nothing to do with national security interests — but we are currently seeing reports that the Pentagon is increasingly concerned about the possibility of our participating in this kind of trade.

We have also recently applied to enter GATT itself, and the American government has said it wouldn't support our membership. I think this should change; I think all these artificial barriers to trade with socialist countries should be eliminated.

JKG: I would agree.

SM: There's no way we can cooperate with western countries in a constructive way until these restrictions are removed.

JKG: Again I agree, and, indeed, I see this as a fruitful area for cooperation. I'm not familiar with the Multifiber Arrangement, but I can't think there would be any great strategic danger in the Soviet Union's becoming aware of our long staple cotton or even our nylon hosiery. Membership in GATT is also something that should be considered. But let me take this a step beyond. To further cooperation, what about Soviet membership in the International Monetary Fund and the World Bank. Do you think that's a possibility?

SM: Mr. Gorbachev recently said quite plainly that we consider ourselves to be part of the world economy, and, as I've indicated before, he also said that one of the aims of our economic reform is to achieve currency convertibility. I don't see how that can be achieved and maintained without the cooperation of the capitalist monetary authorities, including the IMF, in which a number of socialist countries are participating right now.

I must also indicate — and this is a particular feature in which I am interested — that the Soviet Union is a large producer of gold, in fact the second largest producer of gold in the world, and although I know that measures have been taken by the IMF and other bodies in the West to demonetize gold, it's still a significant factor in money markets and in the area of monetary affairs. I think that the Soviet Union would be very much interested in what happens to the price and future of gold.

JKG: The Soviet Union joining the IMF is certainly something we should have in mind and welcome. As to gold, I don't think it is now of great monetary importance. Nor would I like to see it accorded any increase in monetary importance. Gold now serves as a kind of last resort in what is considered an uncertain world, and it is, of course, a great object of speculation. I would be opposed to any steps back to a gold standard or any support to gold prices beyond that now accorded by frightened, nervous people and speculators.

SM: Isn't it true that at one point the Reagan administration considered a return to the gold standard?

JKG: I have said previously in these conversations that I'm not a devout supporter of the economic policies of Mr. Reagan.

Let me also suggest another form of cooperation. That is the avoidance in the future of trade action to compel political action. This, I believe, has been more frequently undertaken by the United States than by the Soviet Union in the past. It hasn't been successful, and I think it stirs an antagonism that is counterproductive. We have already mentioned the wheat embargo, the pipeline sanctions and the Jackson-Vanik bill, which denies most-favored-nation trade to the Soviet Union pending relevant progress on human rights. I am, as I've indicated, a strong supporter of human rights, but I don't think they are achieved that way.

But let me continue to yet another field of what I would hope might be greater cooperation to our mutual advantage. That is the area of scientific and cultural exchanges.

In the past, when people have talked about better relations with the Soviet Union, there has been some tendency to fall back on such exchanges as the least controversial step. Advocacy of cultural exchanges has been the refuge of the slightly bankrupt mind. Nonetheless, I think they're still important. What do you see as our mutual advantage in scientific and cultural exchanges?

SM: The scientific exchange agreement between the United States and the Soviet Union was signed early in 1958 to provide for the exchange of scientists in various fields on a regular basis. Soviet scientists coming to work in American universities and American scientists working in Soviet universities and in the research institutes of the Academy of Sciences.

There are quite a number of people who have been exchanged in these last years, and I must say that the agreement, which was first implemented when my father was ambassador in your country, has been fairly successful. It has survived all the political crises of the last three decades.

I remember that I myself was here on an exchange program in 1962, at the time of the Cuban missile crisis. I was then finishing my book *Millionaires and Managers,* and although the Cuban crisis was very much on everyone's mind at that time, it had absolutely no effect on the scholarly exchange. I think that's a very positive sign.

But I also think that the kind of exchanges envisaged by the agreement are very limited. They only pertain to a small number of scholars working in each country. I think a much wider scientific exchange in crucial areas would be important for both countries and for humanity as a whole.

JKG: Let's pursue that. What are some of the larger and more specific areas in which we might have joint effort?

SM: One is in developing new sources of energy — solar energy, tidal energy, underground sources of energy including hot thermal water, and also nuclear fusion. Nuclear fusion is something that has been explored in both countries for a number of years now, and I must say without great success. Electric plants getting their power from nuclear fusion haven't been practical either in your country or in ours.

JKG: You have in mind what we might do jointly to ensure against another disaster like Chernobyl?

SM: No, I'm talking about a totally new kind of nuclear plant. The plants we have currently in operation use the more conventional sources of atomic power like uranium and its various isotopes. When I talk about nuclear fusion, I mean putting the hydrogen bomb, not the atomic bomb, to work for civilian purposes. Atomic energy power plants are a well-established institution. They should be safer, but they are already producing a large part of the electricity in many countries. The nuclear fusion plant would be based on the hydrogen bomb fusion principle rather than on the atomic bomb fission principle.

JKG: I confess to some doubts about the practicality of this discussion. I think for the moment we should confine ourselves to less monumental things. I become uneasy about any development of quite such profound implications. Couldn't we stick for the time being to medical cooperation? We are both terribly afflicted by the environmental factors that cause cancer. We both have present and potential problems with AIDS. I would like to urge that we stay with those rather than getting into the economic potential of the hydrogen bomb.

SM: You are raising a very important issue. However, the question of safety and security associated with the operation of atomic energy plants is very important too. We are, of course, most grateful for the help your doctors gave us at the time of the Chernobyl disaster. It was a private initiative on the American side supported by one of your leading industrialists, Armand Hammer, but, as I said, it was an instance where we cooperated fully. It also led to more cooperation on our side with the United States and the other countries in the International Atomic Energy Agency in Vienna. There a whole new set of rules was developed to ensure the safety of the atomic reactors presently in operation. But let me get back to the fusion problem just for a second.

Work in this area is now under way in both the United States and the Soviet Union. I agree that there are dangers associated with that kind of energy, but since work is proceeding, there has to be an established system of cooperation. We have to decide whether it's worthwhile going ahead with it. We have to decide what safety procedures must be developed before nuclear fusion goes into use, if it does. We have to decide whether it's necessary to use that source of energy, which, of course, represents an enormous potential for civilization in the future. Do we have to put our brakes on this development? Or should we promote it? I think this isn't something for one of the countries to decide independently. Both countries, and others as well, should decide in cooperation.

JKG: I see your point. But you and I have both sought to keep our discussions very much within the realm of practical action, and I confess to thinking that the management of nuclear fusion is a bit over the margin; it may be too visionary.

SM: It has been a point of discussion between the heads of our governments in recent high-level talks, so it should be considered a practical possibility. And, for that matter, we have approached the French government on the same issues, and although no agreement has yet been reached, at least it's one area in which talks have started.

JKG: On a much more mundane subject, what about a great deal more association in the field of education? I'm rather pleased by the number of American teachers and especially the number of our students who now travel each year to the Soviet Union and the number of your students who visit us. Shouldn't we register our commitment to a lot more cooperation in this area?

sm: I think that's absolutely right. While I've been here this summer, I've met a few teachers in the Vermont area who are planning to go over to the Soviet Union, taking their high school students with them. They're preparing for this visit in great detail, studying the Russian language and culture, very carefully planning the points of interest they would like to visit in Leningrad and Moscow.

I think it's especially important that this kind of exchange continue. Recently a large group of American teachers of the Russian language went over to tour the Soviet Union, and they interested themselves in how foreign languages are being taught in our country. They visited a number of our schools and got real firsthand experience in studying the methods being used.

Close to the end of their tour, they were received by Mr. Gorbachev, which is a sign of the great importance our government accords to this kind of thing. I think there has to be more of it. There has to be more knowledge of each other's culture and of each other's language.

jkg: I must rise in my stalwart way to the defense of President Reagan. Let me note that the other evening he addressed the two hundred and thirty Soviet visitors who came to Chautauqua in upstate New York this summer. This was something I was very pleased to see him do.

Could I now come to something that is much on my mind? That is cooperation in what we might call the age of entertainment. There has been a good deal of discussion in the United States about how we are moving from being an economy based on physical production to being a service economy. I would revise that to say that we have really moved into the era of entertainment. After people have enough goods, they turn to enjoyment — enjoyment in the arts, in music and literature.

Going back to ancient times, Russia has been proud of its artistic achievement, and I would hope that we might have much more benefit from Soviet theater, writing, ballet and the arts in general, with the companion hope that there would be a large flow in the opposite direction.

SM: Yes, I would support that. Although the Soviet people haven't yet reached a point of complete satisfaction as far as material goods are concerned, they have long followed the biblical injunction that man is not satisfied by bread alone. They are interested in reading American literature, listening to American musicians, including jazz and pop artists and more serious classical music, seeing more American movies, attending your opera and your ballet. They want to do that even before they have satisfied their need for food and automobiles.

JKG: You are willing to accept some of our more culturally depraved television, are you?

SM: There is already a lot of exchange in the area of television; I have myself participated in quite a number of American programs.

JKG: Those are at a higher level than the ones to which I was alluding.

SM: It's now a regular feature of Soviet television to carry what are called space bridges, discussions between citizens of Leningrad and Los Angeles or Moscow and Bonn or Tbilisi and Paris. These are examples of what it's technically possible to do in this age of satellite communications.

JKG: I suppose we should also mention tourism, which is, after all, an industry of no slight importance. What possibilities do you see there?

SM: Tourism is rapidly expanding in the Soviet Union. More foreigners are coming to our country as tourists and more Soviet citizens are going abroad. I think that aside from the entertainment and recreational rewards of tourism, the expansion of our knowledge of the relations between countries at the personal level is an important human endeavor.

JKG: What about your currency convertibility? Isn't that going to be necessary before we can have any great flow of Soviet tourists to New York City or Yellowstone Park?

SM: Yes, that's right. At the moment any Soviet citizen who goes abroad as a tourist has the possibility of exchanging an adequate sum of money for his trip, but if the number of tourists were to increase, we would have balance of payments problems. As I've already mentioned, an increase in foreign trade, especially trade with Western areas, would provide more possibilities of exchange with other countries and particularly for tourists.

Now, we can't permit ourselves, as you do in the United States, to have the Japanese underwrite our tourism by buying up our production facilities and our banks, thus providing the money for our citizens to go abroad. You may not be concerned with that, but we fear a possible Japanization or Americanization of our economy. We want to keep our foreign payments in balance.

JKG: So you're going to keep your tourists at home for a while?

SM: No, we are going to expand our tourism. As trade expands, tourism will expand. We're just making it contingent on our competitive capacity in world markets.

JKG: Why don't we foresee an arrangement by which the tourist revenues spent by Americans or Westerners traveling in the Soviet Union are held in escrow to allow the same number of Soviet travelers to go to Western Europe or the United States? We might see this as a separate area of exchange. It would take a bit of planning, but the result would be that the more Americans who travel to Russia — something that I personally have greatly enjoyed — the more money there would be available for Soviet citizens to travel to Western Europe or the United States.

SM: That could be helpful. And may I add that I'm glad that you're beginning, after our discussions, to perceive the benefits of planning.

JKG: I'm not averse to planning.

SM: You should realize, Galbraith, that in order to accommodate more foreign tourists, we will have to build quite a number of hotels and, in fact, increase our road-building program.

JKG: So this is another area where we could have joint ventures, in the building of hotels. Couldn't there be joint ventures with Holiday Inns, the Hilton Hotels, the Marriotts?

SM: Hilton and Marriott hotels presumably will be built in the inner cities, but as far as Holiday Inns are concerned, they have, generally, to be built somewhere along highways. We don't have enough highways right now to allow us to proceed with a Holiday Inn type of enterprise, so one area in which we could also cooperate might be in highway construction.

JKG: I suppose that's true, but the best way we could cooperate would be to urge you to be a little more sensible on this matter. We have built miles of highways in this country at the expense of our once very good railway network, which is now sadly in decline and out of repair. I don't want to offer advice to the socialist world, but I hope you won't make our mistake and give up your railway system for superhighways. I hope that you will continue to invest heavily in your railroads, even at the expense of your roads.

SM: I assure you that we have no intention of eliminating our railroads. If in a few years you still want to go across our country on the Trans-Siberian Express, it will certainly be there waiting for you. But do I understand you to mean that you wouldn't like to take your car on a cross-continental run through the Soviet Union on one of our highways?

JKG: Absolutely not, I have no desire whatsoever to do so. I would enjoy taking the train trip, but I react violently to the thought of a trip from Moscow to Vladivostok on a superhighway.

SM: We will have to see whether the other Americans, the West Europeans and the Japanese would agree with that.

But on another subject: with the increase in the movement of people across borders, we have to be careful about such things as the spread of disease and the spread of drugs into our country.

It's true that in the last two decades the international narcotics traffic has increased enormously. You might be surprised to know that, according to United Nations statistics, every one hundredth man or woman on earth is a drug addict right now — one percent of the total population of the world or fifty million people. That has been made possible by the expansion of underground empires that produce, distribute and sell cocaine, heroin, marijuana, hashish and other drugs across the continents. It has become a multinational trade. We're coming to a point where drugs may become more readily available than potatoes or cucumbers in the farmers' market, and that's a great, great menace, particularly for the younger generation but also for civilization as a whole.

JKG: Surely you're not suggesting that we stop tourist travel in order to control drugs?

SM: No, I'm talking about a different thing. I think we should have more international cooperation, including cooperation between the United States and the Soviet Union, in controlling that particular kind of underground activity.

JKG: I completely agree.

15

Terms of Cooperation:
Final Words

SM: We have been talking about more cooperation in the medical field. I approve of that. The fight against alcoholism is something we take very much to heart in the Soviet Union, and the same is true of drug addiction. My own daughter is now actively participating as a doctor in that particular area, but I feel that the efforts of medical personnel aren't enough. I think there have to be concerted efforts by our governments to curb the underground empires that produce the drugs and are such a great danger to our societies.

JKG: Yes, this is an area of cooperation that very much needs to be explored.

Now, what about joint efforts on behalf of the environment, protection of our oceans, protection of the ozone layer and other things we've already mentioned?

SM: And I would add again the security of nuclear plants.

JKG: So that we don't have the kind of disaster the United States had at Three Mile Island and you had in much greater form at Chernobyl?

SM: I support that absolutely. In fact, our newspapers have recently been pointing to the fact that security arrangements in atomic energy plants in our country have improved in many cases, but they're still lagging dangerously behind in some.

JKG: This is also a matter of grave concern here in the United States, where we have built our nuclear plants not under the stern eye of a larger power authority but under the sometimes very casual and possibly even incompetent management of the local utility companies. We're going to have to do much better in the future than we have done in the past.

SM: There is one other area I would like to talk about, and that is mutual cooperation on exhaustible resources. The supply of mineral resources on the planet is limited. We will be reaching some point in the future — maybe a hundred years ahead, maybe a hundred and fifty, I'm not venturing any exact forecast — when they will become dangerously depleted. That's why we need new sources of energy. That's why we need new sources of raw materials, including superconducting materials and other new substances created by new ventures in science.

We will also have to go jointly into space, to the moon and the other planets, to seek new resources. All of this is necessary. It's also a little in the area of fantasy, as you have indicated before, or, at the least, we don't know exactly what will happen or how. What we do know is that the present mineral resources are going to run out at some point. That's why we should even now get together and start cooperating on projects in the particular field of resource management.

What I have also in mind is the continuing population explosion. Right now we have a little more than five billion people living in the world. At the beginning of the next century, according to United Nations projections, we will have ten billion, and then if we accept its very optimistic forecast, the population of the world will stop increasing by the end of the twenty-first century, when we will have between ten and fifteen billion.

That will be a fairly stable number, but it will be stable only if living standards in the developing countries increase accordingly.

JKG: You're saying that higher living standards remove the pressure to have more children?

SM: That's right; it's a generally accepted fact. There are different forms of population control. We know that some are now particularly successful in China, which has recently officially indicated that it has succeeded in cutting down its population growth. It's keeping it to a certain figure, which, though large, is smaller than it would have been if there had been no such efforts. In the rest of the world, however, population control measures won't necessarily be as successful.

We have a Catch-22 problem here. On the one hand, there is the fact that the population will stabilize at a lower level if living standards increase faster. On the other hand, the more the living standards increase — the more the Third World countries come close to the kind of consumption we have in the Soviet Union or the United States — the more the world's resources will be exhausted. There has to be a universal conscious effort to prepare for the future in terms of protecting our resources.

JKG: I see the need for planning in that area. And I also see the need for contemplating a standard of living that makes less massive withdrawals on exhaustible resources than we do at the moment. Our standard of living is going to have to be accommodated sometime in the future to what is available or can be discovered.

We must always bear in mind that only a handful of countries, including, first of all, the United States, then Japan, Western Europe and the Soviet Union, are now responsible for using up our resources. Maybe the consumer standard of living we enjoy in this part of the world will have to change.

SM: I find that we're in conflict with ourselves here, and it seems to me that it's a real conflict, not just an error in our logic. We talk about the necessity of expanding consumer-oriented economies in other countries, including the socialist countries and presumably the Third World, but then we talk about the necessity of somehow getting away from the kind of consumer society that exists today because it can't be supported indefinitely in its present form by the resources now on the planet. This seems to indicate that civilization doesn't have an easy path before it.

JKG: It's a problem we must address jointly. But let me go on to two other matters.

We have just been speaking of the less fortunate, less developed part of the world. In the short run, there's no question that the most important goal there is to have an improvement in the basic conditions of life — in their living standards. What can both our countries do about it? Let me make a suggestion or two.

Let us first try to correct one of the more disgraceful afflictions for which we are responsible, one I have mentioned before. I have in mind the sale of armaments to the Third World.

SM: I think we've agreed already that that should be controlled. It's something that has yet to be done by our governments, but we have to do it, yes.

JKG: As a second step, we must see that some of the resources now going for military assistance to those countries, the money now being spent for weapons, go instead toward improving and supporting their economic life.

SM: That is something that the United Nations has been proposing and upholding for quite a number of years. We don't seem to be getting closer to agreement on these issues, but recently the Soviet Union has come up with a new suggestion that we use part of the reduction in armament expenditure to provide additional economic assistance to the developing lands. Incidentally, some of the Western countries, including France, have supported our proposal. I am hopeful that at some point it will get support from the government of the United States as well.

JKG: Our government hasn't been particularly forthcoming on this issue in the recent past. I do think, however, that there is a strong popular view in the United States that favors less military aid to a very poor country like Pakistan and much more economic help instead. By diminishing such aid to Pakistan, we would then diminish the seeming need of India to spend money on armaments. Of course, all this, if I may say so, could be helped by your finding a settlement in Afghanistan. The war there is, in some ways, the excuse for putting more arms into that part of the world.

SM: I hope the government of the United States will also be helpful in that matter.

JKG: I hope so too. Now, finally, I want to emphasize something we have discussed before. I think the greatest need of all is for cooperation in the reduction of tension between our two countries. This would lead to an effective arms agreement, one that would go well beyond what is now being discussed. We want to make possible a very large mutual reduction in arms expenditures and the transfer of resources to civilian purposes, both in our own countries and in other, even more needful lands. I see that as the ultimate purpose for our cooperation.

SM: I agree with you, and I see it also as one of the conditions that will affect our eventual full cooperation. If there is a continued armaments race, if there is increased tension, there is no way we can talk meaningfully about a peaceful future for the planet, a future in which all people of all races and all nationalities can cooperate together toward a better world.